Lockheed L-188 Electra

RON MAK

HISTORIC COMMERCIAL AIRCRAFT SERIES, VOLUME 14

Front cover image: Fred Olsen Lockheed L-188 LN-FOG on July 27, 1985. This picture was taken from a Piper Navajo Pa-31 as both aircraft flew over the Netherlands.

Title page image: An Air Bridge Lockheed L-188 at Tuscon in March 1992.

Back cover image: TAME Lockheed L-188 HC-AZL at Guyaquil Airport, Ecuador.

Published by Key Books
An imprint of Key Publishing Ltd
PO Box 100
Stamford
Lincs PE9 1XQ

www.keypublishing.com

The right of Ron Mak to be identified as the author of this book has been asserted in accordance with the Copyright, Designs and Patents Act 1988 Sections 77 and 78.

Copyright © Ron Mak, 2022

ISBN 978 1 80282 486 5

Typeset by SJmagic DESIGN SERVICES, India.

Introduction

Lockheed's first appraisals of the short- and medium-range airliner market were made in the early 1950s, and previous experience with building the C-130 Hercules military transport led the company to build a turboprop rather than a pure jet design. In 1954, it offered American Airlines a high wing design, the CL-303, with four Dart or Eland engines, but this proved too small for American's needs, as did the low-wing, Allison-powered CL-310, which was Lockheed's next proposal. However, in January 1955, American issued its detailed requirements to the US aerospace industry at large, in response to which Lockheed announced a scaled-up development of the CL-310, known as the Lockheed L-188 Electra. American's order for 35 Lockheed L-188 Electras "off the drawing board" was quickly followed by one from Eastern Air Lines for 40 Lockheed L-188 Electras. A year after its announcement, the L-188 Electra had attracted orders for 128 aircraft, and this total had risen to 144 by the time the first prototype was flown in December 1957. A second prototype was flown on February 13, 1958, and a third on August 19, 1958, the latter being used as the US Navy's aerodynamic prototype for the P-3 (then P3V-1) Orion anti-submarine aircraft. On August 22, Federal Aviation Administration (FAA) type certification was granted (at a gross weight of 51,257kg) to the Lockheed L-188A, the initial production version.

The first L-188A (N5501) was delivered to Eastern Air Lines on October 8, 1958, from Lockheed's Burbank plant in California, and put into scheduled operation on January 12, 1959. American Airlines' first L-188A Electra entered service 11 days later. The Lockheed L-188A was supplanted as the standard model by Lockheed L-188C Electra, which had increased fuel capacity and gross weight and seats from 74 (standard) to 99 (high density). The first recipient of the Lockheed L-188C was Northwest Airlines. The only European operator to order was KLM Royal Dutch Airlines, which ordered 12, the first of which was delivered as PH-LLA L-188C *Mercurius* on September 21, 1959, and entered service in December 1959.

A setback to the Lockheed L-188 Electra's career occurred after serious accidents to a Braniff aircraft in September 1959 and a Northwest aircraft in the following March. Speed restrictions were imposed on all in-service Electras until January 1961, while all Lockheed Electra's on the production line and in service underwent a strengthening of the nacelle and surrounding wing structure. In total, 170 production L-188 Electras were built. While this number may not have been as high as Lockheed would have liked, the manufacturer, as well as its many operators, still felt the Lockheed L-188 was a success. Furthermore, despite the intervention of the pure jet age in the form of Douglas and Boeing, around 13 of these US-designed and built turbo-prop airliners still remain in some form of service today.

Ron Mak
Almere, Netherlands
September 29, 2022

Lockheed L-188 Electra

Cathay Pacific Lockheed L-188A VR-HFN at Tokyo Haneda Airport in May 1961. This aircraft was delivered to the Lockheed Aircraft Corporation as N1882 (msn 1002) and sold to Cathay Pacific as VR-HFN on June 29, 1959. It was bought by Ecuatoriana as HC-AMS on March 11, 1967, and then sold to Transportes Aereos Nacionales Ecuatorianos (TAME) as FAE1002/HC-AMS in March 1975. It was seen broken up at Quito Airport in Ecuador in 1981. (Peter Gates Collection)

NASA Lockheed NP-3A N428NA (msn 1003) at Miami International Airport on October 31, 1978. Originally operated by the US Navy with as an XP3V -1/NP-3A, NASA's single Electra is a very extensively instrumented aircraft operated from Houston for the study of magnetic aerodynamic and astronomical observations. It first flew in August 1958. It was on display at the National Museum of Naval Aviation in Pensacola, Florida, as of September 21, 1993.

Lockheed Aircraft Corporation Lockheed L-188A N7144C arrives at Amsterdam Schiphol Airport on October 10, 1958, on a demonstration flight for KLM Royal Dutch Airlines. Originally intended for Aeronaves de Mexico, this aircraft was delivered back to the Lockheed Aircraft Corporation in April 1958 as N1883 (msn 1004) after the order lapsed and was registered as N7144C. The aircraft was bought by Cathay Pacific as VR-HFO on April 1, 1959, and left the Cathay fleet in June 1965. It was sold to General Dynamics Corporation as N16816, then to F. B. Ayer & Associates in May 1966, leased to Braniff on October 12, 1966, till October 1967, and was then bought by Ecuatoriana as HC-ANQ in 1968. It was transferred to TAME as FAE1004/HC-ANQ in March 1975 and was broken up at Quito Airport, Ecuador, during 1981. (Ad Jan Altevogt)

Lockheed Aircraft Corporation Lockheed L-188A N7144C at Amsterdam Schiphol Airport on October 10, 1958. The fourth prototype, N1884, was re-registered as N7144C and used for an around the world demonstration flight for prospective customers and operators on an airline schedule basis. (Ad Jan Altevogt)

Evergreen International Airlines Lockheed L-188A N1006T at Oakland Airport, California, in October 1976. This aircraft was delivered to General Motors Corporation as N5501V (msn 1006) in July 1958 and was re-registered as N1R on April 1961, later being sold to the Los Angeles Dodgers in November of that year. It was sold on to American Airlines on December 17, 1970, as N1432 and was withdrawn from use (wfu) at Oklahoma Airport in 1971. It was bought by Intermountain Aviation as N90700 on January 28, 1972, and re-registered as N1006T in March of that year. The aircraft was then sold to Johnson International Airlines on March 1, 1975, which merged with Evergreen International Airlines on October 31, 1975. Originally known as Evergreen Helicopters, this company entered the airline business with the purchase of Johnson Flying Service and Intermountain Aviation in 1975. A new subsidiary of Evergreen International was set up, with main operating bases at Marana in Arizona and Missoula in Montana. Evergreen specializes in both passenger and light cargo charters, and also carries out a large amount of contract work for the US Forest Service during the annual fire-fighting season in the US, carrying fire crews and high-priority cargo. Evergreen's first three Electras arrived in October 1975, and N1006T was sold to Air California in March 1977 as N125AC. (Michel Anciaux)

Air California Lockheed L-188A N125AC at Orange County Airport, California, on November 28, 1978. Air California began operations on January 17, 1967, with two Electras from American Airlines on a San Francisco to Orange County Airport route. With expansion, two more Electras were purchased from Qantas. Points served eventually included Oakland, San José, Burbank, San Diego, Palm Springs, Ontario and Sacramento. With the collapse of Holiday Airlines in 1975, Air California purchased one of Holiday's Electras and was subsequently awarded the defunct airline's Northern California routes.

Mandala Airlines Lockheed L-188C PK-RLF at Jakarta-Kemayoran Airport in August 1984. Mandala Airlines was formed in April 1969 and started with three Vickers Viscounts on domestic routes; these aircraft were replaced by six Lockheed Electras between 1979 and 1983. PK-RLF was bought from Air California in October 1980, was wfu in 1993 and left the fleet in June 1995. It was later converted to a tanker aircraft and re-registered as C-FVFH with Air Spray in Canada and was still active in 2022. (R.M Collection)

Air Manila Lockheed L-188A RP-C1061 at Manila International Airport in May 1976. Delivered to Eastern Airlines on October 8, 1958, as N5502 (msn 1007), this aircraft was bought by Air Manila on December 1, 1971, and re-registered as RP-C1061. Air Manila was formed in February 1964, providing flights with its two DC3s, and with H.P. Heralds, Fairchild F27s, Lockheed L-188As and Boeing 707s. During a flight from Wake Island to Manila, on June 4, 1976, the aircraft made a maintenance stop at Agana Naval Air Station (Guam). Shortly after the work was completed, the L-188A took off for Manila, but just after take-off the number 3 engine failed and struck the rising terrain, causing the aircraft to come to rest near a residential area and burst into flames. (Pierre-Alan Petit)

Copa Panama Lockheed L-188A HP-579 at Panama Tocumen Airport on November 15, 1971. Originally delivered to Eastern Airlines as N5506 (msn 1011) on November 3, 1958, it was sold to Copa Panama on October 17, 1971. Copa Panama, officially Compania Panamena de Aviacion SA, was founded on June 21, 1944, with the assistance of Pan American Airways, which provided 40 percent of the capital. Services began over local routes in August 1947 from Panama City with a Douglas DC3 and later with a Convair 440 and HS-748. Copa began to acquire Electras in 1971, and two more were bought in 1974 to fill expanded capacity needs and fly new routes to Managua, San José, San Salvador and Bogota.

Eastern Airlines Lockheed L-188A N5507 at New York La Guardia Airport on July 5, 1973. This aircraft (msn 1012) was first flown on November 9, 1958, and was delivered to Eastern Airlines on November 14 of the same year from the Lockheed Air Terminal at Burbank Airport in California. It was stored between use at Fort Lauderdale Airport in Florida from 1970; it was then bought by Zantop International Airlines on February 22, 1978, and flown to Detroit Ypsilanti Airport in Michigan for freighter conversion. The aircraft was sold to Turboprop Ventures in Anaheim, California, in July 2006 as N5507 and was wfu and scrapped at Willow Run Airport in Michigan in 2007.

SAM Colombia Lockheed L-188A HK-553 at El Dorado Airport, Bogota, on March 29, 1975. Delivered to Eastern Airlines as N5509 (msn 1013) on November 29, 1958, this aircraft was out of service in August 1969 and stored at Fort Lauderdale Airport. It was bought by SAM Colombia on October 22, 1969, as HK-553 and was then returned to the US (repossessed) in March 1977. It was later reissued as N5509Y, having been bought by American Jet Industries on October 13, 1977. It was wfu and stored at Van Nuys Airport in California, later being broken up in January 1980. (R.M Collection)

Zantop International Airlines Lockheed L-188AF N5510L at Willow Run Airport, Michigan, on April 22, 1980. The aircraft was originally delivered to Eastern Airlines as N5510 (msn 1014) on January 13, 1959, and left the fleet in August 1969. It was bought by SAM Colombia on December 29, 1969, as HK-557 and returned to the US (repossessed) to join Eastern Airlines as N5510L in March 1977. It was bought by American Jet Industries on November 14, 1977, and was sold to Zantop International Airlines on March 14, 1978, and converted to L-188AF standard in January 1979. On September 7, 2006, the aircraft was bought by Turboprop Ventures LLC, Anaheim, California, and then sold on January 31, 2013, to a company in Crofton, Maryland.

Servicio Aereo De Honduras SA (SAHSA) Lockheed L-188A HR-SAW at New Orleans Airport, Louisiana, on July 15, 1973. The aircraft was delivered to Eastern Airlines on December 16, 1958, as N5513 (msn 1018). It was bought by Winner Airways from Taiwan as B-3057 on April 6, 1970, but was returned to Eastern Airlines on June 16, 1970, and sold to SAHSA Honduras on December 9, 1970, as HR-SAW *Copan Galel*. SAHSA was established on March 8, 1945, with the help of Pan American Airways, which provided 40 percent of the capital. Operations started on October 22, with Douglas DC-3s flying between Tegucigalpa and San Pedro Sula (Honduras). (R.M Collection)

SAHSA Lockheed L-188A HR-SAW arrives at the Tegucigalpa Toncontin Airport in a new striking color scheme on April 29, 1976. On January 8, 1981, SAHSA's Lockheed L-188A Electra arrived with one engine shutdown at Guatemala La Aurora Airport from Tegucigalpa Toncontin Airport, and the crew decided to ferry the aircraft to Honduras for repairs without passengers. The crew took off for a three-engined ferry flight to Tegucigalpa, but shortly after take-off, the pilot reported a total loss of hydraulic pressure and difficulty in controlling the aircraft. The L-188A began to return to Guatemala La Aurora Airport, but the aircraft lost altitude then crashed into houses one mile west of the airport. Six crew members were killed, however, although the L-188A crashed in a densely populated urban area, there were no fatalities on the ground. (R.M Collection)

Blue Airlines Lockheed L-188A 9Q-CDK *Lodja Putu* is wfu at N'Djili Airport, Kinshasa, on February 21, 1995. Originally delivered to American Airlines on January 4, 1959, as N6103A with msn 1024, this aircraft was in service till March 1962 before being bought by Brazilian Airline Varig on September 10, 1962, as PP-VJL. It was wfu at Sao Paulo Congonhas Airport in December 1991, later being sold to Blue Airlines of the Democratic Republic of the Congo on July 29, 1993, as 9Q-CDK. Blue had a fleet of four Lockheed L-188A Electras: 9Q-CDG, 9Q-CDI, 9Q-CDK, and 9Q-CDL. (Michel Anciaux)

Varig Lockheed L-188A PP-VJM at Congonhas Airport, Sao Paulo, on October 24, 1988. Delivered to American Airlines on January 9, 1959, as N6104A (msn 1020), the aircraft was named *Flagship Washington*. It left American Airlines in March 1962 and was bought by Varig on August 30, 1962, as PP-VJM. After 30 years, it left the fleet and was preserved at the Museu Aeroespacial at Campo dos Afonsos, near Rio de Janeiro, in full Varig colors.

US Navy Lockheed L-188A N5518 at Kwajalein Missle Range (Los Angeles Airport) in 1977. Delivered to Eastern Airlines on February 14, 1959, as N5518 (msn 1026), the aircraft left Eastern Airlines in May 1977 and was leased to the US Navy on July 8, 1977. It was returned on March 10, 1981. It was then bought by Atlas Aircraft Corporation and sold to Mandala Airlines of Indonesia as PK-RLH in January 1983, later being wfu and stored at Jakarta Airport in September 1989. In July 1995, it was bought by Air Spray of Canada and used for spare parts for its Lockheed L-188A fleet. (R.M Collection)

Honduras Air Force Lockheed L-188A FAH-555 at Miami Airport in August 1979. This aircraft was originally delivered to American Airlines as N6106A *Flagship Dallas* with msn 1028 on January 27, 1959. It was bought by McCulloch International Airlines on November 23, 1971, and leased to Pacific Airlines from April to June 1975. Ownership transferred to Pacific Airlines on January 18, 1978. The aircraft was sold to Honduras Air Force as FAH-555 in August 1979, and it was transferred to the Honduran government as HR-EMA in April 1992. It was bought by Air Spray of Canada as C-GNPB on October 25, 2011, and stored at Red Deer Airport, Alberta.

Lineas Aereas Paraguayas (LAP) Lockheed L-188A ZP-CBX at Asuncion Airport, Paraguay, on January 27, 1979. Originally delivered to Eastern Airlines on March 12, 1959, as N5521 (msn 1032), this aircraft was leased to Overseas National Airways (ONA) in July 1968 and returned on October 4, 1968. It was bought by LAP on February 18, 1969, as ZP-CBX. Three Electras had been purchased at the beginning of December 1968 to serve routes to Brazil, Uruguay, Argentina, Peru and Bolivia in place of the airline's aging Convair 240s.

Above left: LAP Lockheed L-188A ZP-CBX at Asuncion Airport. The interior holds 66 passengers, plus room for a six-person VIP lounge and five-person crew. (Michel Anciaux)

Above right: LAP Lockheed L-188A ZP-CBX at Asuncion Airport. This image shows the Electra interior with a VIP six-seat lounge. (Michel Anciaux)

Right: The cockpit of this LAP Lockheed L-188A is so wide that two sets of throttles are required. (Michel Anciaux)

Guyana Airways Lockheed L-188PF 8R-GEW at Miami Airport, Florida, on July 5, 1977. Delivered to National Airlines on April 1, 1959, as N5001K (msn 1035), this aircraft left the fleet in December 1968 and was leased to Trans Arctic and converted to L-188PF standard. It was sold to Pacific Western Airlines as CF-PWG in April 1972 and bought by MCA Leasing Corporation as N415MA in April 1976. It was later leased to Guyana Airways on October 20, 1976, as 8R-GEW, being returned on September 20, 1977, and subsequently leased to Hawaiian Airlines in March 1978 as N341HA until August 1980. It was leased to Zantop International Airlines on September 2, 1980, and bought by the company in April 1985. It was then leased to Channel Express in August 1992 and returned to Zantop in January 1994 to be stored at Willow Run Airport. It was re-registered as part of the Turboprop Ventures LLC fleet on September 12, 2006. (R.M Collection)

Hawaiian Airlines Lockheed L-188PF N415MA at Willow Run Airport in October 1977. Hawaiian Air Cargo was based at Macon Airport in Georgia and operated eight Lockheed Electras as freighters for military and charter work.

Aeroservicios de California Lockheed L-188A XA-FAM at Miami Airport on February 27, 1973. Delivered to Eastern Airlines as N5524 (msn 1036), this aircraft was bought by Aeroservicios de Califonia as XA-FAM on December 18, 1972. On May 1, 1979, it was sold to Morgan Rourke Aircraft Sales as N83MR. Cardinal Corporation then bought the L-188A on December 12, 1979, and it was sold to Northwest Territorial Airways as C-FNWY in June 1981. It was leased to Air Bridge Carriers in January 1991 until March 12, 1991, and was sold on that date to JBQ Aviation as N3209A. (R.M Collection)

Air Bridge Lockheed L-188A N3209A at Tucson International Airport, Arizona, on April 6, 1992. This aircraft was leased to Indian Ocean Airlines, a short-lived Australian carrier, from JBQ Aviation as VH-IOB on August 14, 1992. The airline intended to fly the L-188A on a Perth to Cocos Island and Christmas Island route, but the service never operated, and the L-188A flew back to the US on December 15, 1992. It returned to JBQ Aviation as N351Q and was stored at Roswell Air Centre in New Mexico in January 1993. It was bought by Air Spray Canada on August 26, 2002, as C-GZVM.

Air Spray Canada Lockheed L-188A C-GZVM at Red Deer Airport on October 8, 2004. This aircraft is still active in 2022. (John Olafson)

Blue Airlines Lockheed L-188A 9Q-CDI at N'Djili Airport on February 27, 1998. This aircraft American Airlines *Flagship Buffalo* N6108A with msn 1037 was delivered on February 16, 1959. It left the American Airlines' fleet after being bought by Varig on September 10, 1962, as PP-VJN and was leased to Cruzeiro do Sul from March to April 1975. It was returned to Varig and in 1992 was reported to be stored at Porto Alegre. The aircraft was bought by Blue Airlines as 9Q-CDI in June 1993 and was leased to the Congolese Armed Forces to transport fuel to Mbandaka. Readied for a flight on February 8, 1999, the Electra was six tonnes overload and carrying fuel, bombs and ammunition. It was staffed by the captain, flight engineer and ground enginner. During take off, engine number 3 had to be shut down. The captain tried to return to the airport, but the Electra lost altitude, crashing some three minutes after take-off near N'Djili Airport. (Michel Anciaux)

Ansett Airlines of Australia Air Cargo Lockheed L-188AF VH-RMA at Kingford Smith Airport, Sydney, in April 1978. This aircraft was delivered to Ansett Airlines on February 27, 1959, as VH-RMA (msn 1039), and was converted to L-188AF freighter standard in July 1972.

Ansett Air Freight Lockheed L-188AF VH-RMA at Melbourne Tullamarine Airport. The company's first three Lockheed L-188A's (VH-RMA (msn 1039)), VH-RMC (msn 1044)), and VH-RMB (msn 1047)) were used for domestic services until 1971, when the availability of jet equipment spelled the end of the turboprop supremacy. With this in mind, Ansett contracted Lockheed to convert all three to freighters. These were so successful in service that a fourth aircraft was obtained in 1975 and also converted by Lockheed in August 1975 as VH-RMG (msn 1123). (R.M Collection)

Air Bridge Lockheed L-188AF N356Q at Southend Airport, UK, in April 1989. The aircraft was bought from Ansett in October 1984 by TPI International Airways as N356Q (msn 1039) and leased to Air Bridge Carriers on February 10, 1988. It was re-registered as N355WS on November 23, 1989, and returned to TPI on December 21, 1990. It was subsequently sold to JBQ Aviation on April 8, 1992, as N356Q, which leased it to Renown Aviation, and Hunting Cargo Airlines. On November 6, 1996, it was leased to Amerer Air as OE-ILB and was later bought by TNT on August 22, 1998. It was reported as being wfu in June 2002.

Buffalo Airways Lockheed L-188AF C-FBAQ at Yellowknife Airport, Northwest Territories, in July 2007. This aircraft was bought by Buffalo Airways on October 27, 2006, as C-FBAQ and was still active as a tanker in 2022. (Harry Sluyter)

Above: TAME Lockheed L-188A HC-AZT at Guayaquil Airport, Ecuador, November 28, 1977. This aircraft was originally delivered to Braniff Airways on April 29, 1959, as N9701C (msn 1040) Braniff had 11 operational Electras for its short-haul routes in the southern United States. N9701C left the fleet in March 1969 and was bought by F. B. Ayers & Associates on May 26, 1970. It was leased to the US Department of the Interior from 1970 to 1972 and subsequently bought by TAME as HC-AZT on February 27, 1975. TAME is a branch of the Ecuadorean Air Force, which was set up in 1962 to provide domestic passenger and cargo services and fly supplemental routes within Ecuador that commercial airlines found uneconomical.

Right: TAME Lockheed L-188A HC-AZT, having flown from Quito to Guayaquil Airport on November 28, 1977.

Filair Lockheed L-188A 9Q-CDU at Calgary Airport on June 3, 1994. This is ex-HC-AZT, which was bought by Varig on April 1986 as PP-VNK, and stored at Porto Alegre In January 1992. It was sold to Filair on November 1, 1993, as 9Q-CDU and stored at Calgary. The aircraft was later bought by Air Spray Canada in March 1994 as C-GBKT, being re-registered as C-GFQA in November 1999. It crashed on July 16, 2003, near Cranbrook, British Colombia, whilst firefighting after the pilots flew into a ridge. Both crew members lost their lives. (R.M Collection)

Zantop International Airlines Lockheed L-188AF N346HA at Willow Run Airport in August 1980. Delivered to Eastern Airlines as N5527 (msn 1043) on April 16, 1959, this aircraft left the fleet in January 1970. It was then bought by SAM Colombia as HK-691 *Apollo* on November 27, 1970. (Michel Anciaux)

SAM Colombia Lockheed L-188A HK-691 at Panama Tocumen Airport on December 10, 1973. This aircraft was repossessed and returned to Eastern Airlines on March 23, 1977, as N99583 and sold to Aeroservicios de California in April 1977 as XA-SAM. It was then sold to American Jet Industries as N61AJ on February 7, 1978, later being converted to L-188AF standard in April 1978. Bought by Hawaiian Airlines on November 14, 1978, it was sold to Zantop International Airlines on September 2, 1980, and re-registered on June 27, 1985, as N346HA. It was then leased to TMC Airlines from November 1998 until November 2005, after which it was bought by Turboprop Ventures on September 7, 2006. It was sold to Rockland Aerospace Inc on September 29, 2009, and was wfu and stored at Keystone Heights Airpark in Florida.

Ansett Airlines Lockheed L-188A VH-RMB arrives at Kingsford Smith Airport, Sydney, in March 1960. First flown on February 28, 1959, this aircraft was delivered on April 1, 1959, as VH-RMB (msn 1047). Ansett converted the first three Lockheed Electras to freighters (msn 1039, 1044 and 1047) in October 1972. Bought by TPI International Airways in September 1984 as N358Q, it was leased to Fred Olsen Flyveselskap from December 1985 till October 1986. (Peter Gates Collection)

ALM Antillean Airlines Lockheed L-188AF N358Q at Miami Airport in July 26, 1988. It was leased from TPI International Airways from May 1988 to April 1992 and was re-registered as N358WS in October 1989. Stored at Opa Locka Airport, Florida, on January 19, 1996, the aircraft was broken up in March 1997. ALM Antillean Airlines was based at Curacao, the Netherlands; formerly a subsidiary of KLM, it was established on August 1, 1964, to take over the services of the West Indies division of KLM, which had opened a service between Curacao and the neighbouring island of Aruba on January 19, 1935. The new company began operations with Douglas DC-9-15s and 32s on August 1, 1964, and provided services to Aruba, Bonaire, St. Maarten and Suriname and several destinations in the Caribbean such as Puerto Rico, Santo Domingo and Trinidad. Cargo flights from Curacao to Miami were mainly done with leased aircraft such as Douglas DC-6Bs, and later Lockheed L-188AFs were used. (R.M Collection)

Mexican Air Force Lockheed L-188A TP-04 at Miami Airport on February 12, 1978. First flown on April 15, 1959, and delivered to American Airlines as N6112A with msn 1051 on April 22, 1959, this aircraft left the American Airlines fleet in June 1970 and was sold to Oklahoma Airmotive on June 8, 1970. It was bought by the Banco de Mexico in 1975 as XC-HDA, then sold to the Mexican government as XC-UTA in 1977 and transferred to the Mexican Air Force as TP-04 in early 1978. It was re-serialled as TP-201 on February 3, 1979, and re-registered as XC-UTA in March 1980. It was converted to L-188-P(F) standard and was wfu and stored at Singapore Seletar Airport in December 1987. (R.M Collection)

Universal Trading Corporation Lockheed L-188A N9702C at Marana Air Park, Arizona, in September 1973. First flown on March 16, 1959, this aircraft was delivered to Braniff as N9702C (msn 1052) on May 6, 1959. It was bought by Crocker Citizens National Bank on March 28, 1968, and leased back to Braniff Airways on the same date. It was returned to the Crocker Citizens National Bank on March 27, 1969, and was bought by Boeing on February 10, 1971, and stored at Wichita Airport, Kansas. It was sold to Universal Trading Corporation on April 19, 1975, and was bought by TAME in June 1975 as HC-AZY. (R.M Collection)

TAME Lockheed L-188A HC-AZY/FAE1052 at Guayaquil Airport on November 28, 1977. It was bought from Universal Trading Corporation in June 1975 as HC-AZY/FAE1052. During a flight from Lago Agrio to Quito, engine number 2 became inoperative due to technical problems, and the crew decided to take off on a positioning flight to the Capitol of Quito with only three engines. Shortly after take-off from Lago Agrio Airport, while in initial climb, engine number 1 caught fire and exploded. The crew lost control of the Electra, which banked and crashed, bursting into flames. All seven occupants were killed.

ANHSA Carga Lockheed L-188A(F) HR-ANE at Miami Airport on April 21, 1984. Originally delivered to Eastern Airlines on June 2, 1959, as N5532 with msn 1060, the aircraft left the fleet in May 1969. Bought by SAHSA from Honduras as HR-SAV in June 1969, it was leased to TAN Airlines from March to April 1976. It was then converted to L-188A(F) standard in 1977 and leased to ANSHA Carga as HR-ANE in 1984, returning to TAN Airlines as HR-TNT in November 1984. TAN was merged with SAHSA Carga on January 11, 1991, and the aircraft was re-registered as HR-SHN In January 1992. It was bought by Conair Canada on April 14, 1997, as C-FZCS. (R.M Collection)

Conair Lockheed L-188A(F) C-FZCS at Abbotsford, British Columbia, in June 1999. Canadian operator Conair of Abbotsford obtained msn 1060 from ANSHA Honduras on April 14, 1997, and attached a 3,000-gallon tank to the Electra, which was also used on Conair's fire-bomber DC-6s. Air Spray Canada bought the L-188A(F) on March 14, 2000, and it was still active as of 2012. (Ad Jan Altevogt)

Trans Australia Airlines (TAA) Lockheed L-188A VH-TLA *John Eyre* at Brisbane Airport on October 12, 1968. TAA placed its first Electra order on October 10, 1958, with options for another aircraft on October 10, 1958, and another on February 26, 1960. The Electras were used to replace the Douglas DC-6s on TAA domestic route system. The first aircraft was delivered on June 15, 1959, as VH-TLA (msn 1061). This aircraft was bought by Concare Aircraft Leasing Corporation as N188LA on March 12, 1972; it was then leased to Royal Air Lao in May 1972 as XW-PKA. (Ron Cuskelly)

XW-PKA Royal Air Lao Lockheed L-188A at Bangkok Don Muang Airport in December 1972. Two Electras, XW-PKA (msn 1061) and XW-PKB (msn 1069), were leased from Concare Aircraft Leasing Corporation from May 1972 to May 1973 to supplement the single Caravelle in use, for both overseas and domestic routes. Regular services were flown to Saigon, Bangkok and Hong Kong, and the Electras flew numerous domestic routes in support of Royal Air Lao's Douglas DC-4s and Douglas Dc-6s. The airline disappeared in its old form when Laos was overrun by Communist forces. Concare converted it to an L-188A(F) in December 1973 as N188LA. It was bought by American Jet Industries in 1975, flown to Singapore Seletar Airport in March 1976, wfu and broken up in 1976. (R.M Collection)

Varig Lockheed L-188A PP-VLX at Gongonhas Airport, Sao Paulo, on October 24, 1988. Delivered to American Airlines on June 4, 1959, as N6116A (msn 1063) *Flagship Cincinnati*, it left the fleet in January 1971. The aircraft was bought by Aerocondor Colombia on January 12, 1971, as HK-1416 and was sold to Varig in November 1976 as PP-VLX. It left the Varig fleet after 16 years of service and was stored in January 1992. PP-VLX was purchased by Air Spray Canada as C-FQYB in November 1993, but it was written off during a hangar fire at Red Deer Regional Airport on October 26, 2000.

A close-up of Varig Lockheed L-188A PP-VLX before boarding at Santos Dumont Airport, Rio de Janeiro, on October 24, 1988. Mainly used within Brazil, this aircraft also performed the "Flight of Friendship" linking Rio de Janeiro to Lisbon, with a stop in Recife and Sal Island (Cabo Verde). The first flight to Lisbon was inaugurated by a different aircraft, PP-VJO, on November 22, 1965.

Aerocondor Colombia Lockheed L-188A HK-1416, seen at El Dorado Airport on January 15, 1975, was bought from American Airlines on January 12, 1971. Five Lockheed Electras were originally purchased from American Airlines to form the nucleus of a turbine passenger fleet. Services were originally operated to Miami, Bogota, Medellin, Cali, Aruba and other points. Two freighters, HK-774 and HK-1845, were eventually acquired to handle expanding cargo traffic. After six years, HK-1416 was sold to Varig as PP-VLX.

TAN Airlines Lockheed L-188A HR-TNN arriving at Juan Santamaria Airport, San José, on November 10, 1980. Originally delivered to Braniff as N9703C on June 6, 1959, (msn 1067) it was sold to Crocker Citizens National Bank on March 28, 1968, and leased to Braniff Airways on March 28, 1968, and returned on March 27, 1969. It was bought by Boeing on November 9, 1970, and was stored at Wichita Airport Kansas. It was then sold to TAN Honduras on December 17, 1970, as HR-TNN. TAN Airlines flies a route network extending through Central America from the capitol, Tegucigalpa, to Miami, and did so with three Lockheed Electras, HR-SAV, HR-TNN and HR-TNL. TAN sold HR-TNN to the Argentine Navy as 6-P-102 on November 6, 1982, and it was converted to an L-188E at the Central Aeronaval Workshop in October 1984. The L-188 was then stored at Trelew Naval Base on May 14, 1998, with a total of 38,700 flight hours. On November 29, 2021, it was moved to the Almirante Zar Base Aeroclub next to the Base and used by students for rescue and survival practice and cabin crew training.

TAN Airlines Lockheed L-188A HR-TNN arriving at Panama Tocumen Airport on November 11, 1980.

Eastern Airlines Lockheed L-188A N5535 above Miami Airport on July 12, 1973. Delivered to Eastern Airlines on July 9, 1959, as N5535 (msn 1035), it was sold to American Jet Industies on November 30, 1977, and converted to an L-188AF in January 1978. It was bought by Evergreen International Airlines in April 1978, was leased to Combs Freightair from October 30, 1979 to March 1980, then returned to Evergreen. It was then leased to Galaxy Airlines from May 1985 to May 1987, before being sold to Channel Express as EI-CHO on October 10, 1990. It was re-registered as G-CHNX on November 1, 1994, and was wfu and stored on October 5, 1999. The majority of the aircraft was scrapped at Bournemouth Airport, UK, but the nose section moved to Pershore and preserved; it was later given to the Midland Air Museum in Coventry. (R.M Collection)

TACA Air Cargo Lockheed L-188AF YS-07C at Miami Airport on October 15, 1976. Delivered to TAA on July 14, 1959 as VH-TLB, it was wfu and stored on April 1971. It was then bought by Concare Aircraft Leasing Corporation on March 1, 1972, as N188LB, and leased to Royal Air Lao as XW-PKB in May 1972. It returned to Concare Aircraft Leasing in July 1973 and was then sold to American Jet Industries in 1975, later being converted to L-188AF standard in April 1976. It was bought by TACA Air Cargo as YS-07C in May 1976. After a fuel tank exploded during engine start, the subsequent fire destroyed the right wing of the L-188AF at San Salvador Airport in El Salvador on February 2, 1980, and the aircraft was written off. (R.M Collection)

Copa Panama Lockheed L-188C HP-654 at Panama Tocumen Airport in January 1979. First flown on July 21, 1959, the aircraft was originally delivered to Eastern Airlines on July 27, 1959, as N5536 (msn 1071). It was bought by International Air Leases Inc on May 30, 1974, and leased to Copa Panama as HP-654 on June 27, 1974, later being bought by Copa Panama on September 11, 1974. It was sold to WKB Aviation Inc on April 17, 1981, as N511PS but was wfu and stored at Fort Lauderdale Airport in the same month. It was sold to the Argentine Navy on November 2, 1982, and stored at Base Aeronaval Comandante Espora located in Bahia Blanca, Argentina, to be broken up for parts.

Argentine Navy Lockheed L-188PF 6-P-104/1072 at Base Aeronaval Comandante Espora, Bahia Blanca, on July 26, 2008. Originally delivered to American Airlines as N6118A (msn 1072) on July 25, 1959, the aircraft was bought by McCulloch Properties on May 15, 1968, and sold to Pacific Southwest Airlines (PSA) in December 1977. It was bought by Evergreen International Airlines in February 1979 and was re-registered as N5534 and converted to L-188PF in August 1983. It was bought by the Argentine Navy as 6-P-104 on September 9, 1983. (Carlos Abella)

Argentine Navy Lockheed L-188PF 6-P-104/1072 at Base Aeronaval Comandante Espora. It was assigned to the Naval Air Exploration Squadron and converted in 1993 to be an electronic intelligence (ELINT) aircraft designated *Projecto Wave*. These upgrade modifications were most likely done in Israel. The aircraft's last flight with the navy was on October 28, 2002, with a total of 34,581 flight hours. It was later transferred to the Naval Aviation Museum in Bahia Blanca. (Carlos Abella)

PSA Lockheed L-188A N6118A at San Francisco Airport in January 1978. It was bought by the Argentine Navy in September 1993. (R.M Collection)

Aerocondor Colombia Lockheed L-188A HK-775 at El Dorado Airport on November 14, 1969, with a busy background of Colombian Air Force propliners. This aircraft was delivered to American Airlines as N6119A on August 1, 1959, and left the fleet after being bought by Page Leasing Corporation on September 18, 1969. It was then directly sold to Aercondor Colombia as HK-775, and it remained in service until October 1976. It was later sold to Varig in December 1976 as PP-VLY. (R.M Collection)

Trans Service Airlift (TSA) Lockheed L-188A 9Q-CRM at N'djili Airport on February 27, 1998. This aircraft was bought from Varig as PP-VLY by New ACS in November 1992 and re-registered as 9Q-CRM. It was then purchased by TSA in October 1993. TSA was an airline based at N'djili Airport, and was privately owned and operated from 1991 to 1998. For its operations, the company used several types of airliners, such as two Boeing 727-25s, two Vickers Viscount, two Bae (HS) 748s, an Antonov 32A, and three Lockheed L-188As (9Q-CCV, 9Q-CRM, and 9Q-CRR). In 2000, 9Q-CRM was sold to the Air Transport Office as 9Q-CTO and was wfu at N'Djili Airport. (Michel Anciaux)

Johnson International Airlines Lockheed L-188A N7137C at Missoula Airport, Montana, in September 1973. Delivered to Western Airlines as N7137C on July 29, 1959, with msn 1974, this aircraft left the Western Airlines fleet in November 1970 and was bought by Concare Aircraft Leasing Corporation on November 27, 1970. It was leased to Johnson Flying Service on July 25, 1972, and on October 31, 1975, the company was bought out by Evergreen International. The aircraft was converted to L-188AF standard in September 1980 it re-registered as N5558 in August 1981. It was wfu and stored at Marana Air Park in May 1983 and used for spares, and its registration was cancelled in June 1988. (R.M Collection)

Falconair Sweden Lockheed L-188C SE-FGC at London Gatwick Airport on January 4, 1970. Delivered to Eastern Airlines as N5537 (msn 1075) on August 13, 1959, the aircraft left Eastern Airlines and was sold to Falconair Sweden on September 16, 1969, as SE-FGC. A newly formed company, Falconair began operations in January 1969 with passenger charters. Traffic did not meet expectations, and operations ceased in November 1970. Its three Electras were sold or repossessed.

Sterling Airways Sweden Lockheed L-188C SE-FGC at Copenhagen Kastrup Airport on December 5, 1970. Sterling Airways Sweden bought the Electra on November 9, 1970, as SE-FGC. Sterling Airways of Denmark formed a Swedish subsidiary in 1969 to provide holiday charters from Swedish cities. SE-FGC was obtained from the defunct Falconair Sweden company and was operated for two years on these charters before being sold to the US company Air Holiday on March 2, 1973, as N64405. It was then bought by L&S Leasing on March 13, 1973, and was leased to Air Florida and Southeast Airlines. It was converted to L-188CF standard in November 1978 and bought by Hawaiian Airlines on December 1, 1978, as N423MA. (R.M Collection)

Channel Express Lockheed L-188CF N347HA at Southend Airport in November 1990. Hawaiian Airlines bought this aircraft in December 1978 and re-registered it as N347HA on March 25, 1979. It was sold to Zantop International Airways on September 2, 1980, and bought by the Wilmington Trust Company in November 1989. It was leased to Channel Express Air Services on November 30, 1989, and was re-registered as G-OFRT on October 29, 1991. It was wfu at Coventry Airport in the UK in 2003 and was later scrapped. (Clive Head)

ONA Lockheed L-188AF N280F at Willow Run Airport in May 1972. Delivered to National Airlines as N5004K with msn 1076 on August 6, 1959, this aircraft left the ONA fleet in March 1968 and was bought by Pan Aero International Corporation on March 4, 1968. It was subsequently leased back to ONA on the same day, and was then converted to L-188AF standard in September 1968 as N280F *Resolute*. It was later bought back by ONA on December 31, 1968, and renamed *Pegasus*. It was sold to Concare Aircraft Leasing Corporation on July 17, 1974, and was then bought by Integrity Aircraft Sales Inc on July 19, 1974, and leased to Fleming International Airways on the same date. During a flight from Saint Louis International Airport to Willow Run Airport on July 6, 1977, the autofeathering of the number 2 engine forced the crew to abandon the take-off. The Electra was taxied back to the ramp, and maintenance was performed. The second take-off was performed with the number 2 engine at or below flight idle. The Electra lifted off after a ground roll of 8,000ft, veered left and struck the ground near the runway; all three crew members were killed. (R.M Collection)

Fiesta Air Lockheed L-188C N300GA at Long Beach Airport, California, on June 22, 1972. Originally delivered to Northwest Orient Airlines (NWO) on July 29, 1959, as N122US (msn 1077). The aircraft was bought by American Flyers Airline on June 14, 1966, and was sold to Holiday Airlines on January 21, 1970, as N300GA. It was then bought by Fiesta Air on September 8, 1971, and was re-registered as N300FA on October 10, 1972, later being sold to Aviation Equipment Leasing Inc on April 26, 1973. One month later, it was bought by FM Productions Inc on May 4, 1973, and re-registered as N42FM. (Peter de Groot)

FM Productions Lockheed L-188C N42FM *SANTANA* at Melbourne Airport Australia in August 1973. The Electra visited Australia while transporting legendary guitarist Carlos Santana and his band on a tour of the Far East, Australia and New Zealand. It was bought by American Jet Industries Inc on September 5, 1974, and was converted to L-188CF standard in April 1975 and bought by Aerocosta Colombia as HK-1809 *El Caribe* on October 7, 1975. It was sold to Aerocondor Colombia as HK-1845 in March 1976 and was wfu at Barranquilla Airport in 1979 and later broken up. (Mike Madden)

LAP Lockheed L-188C ZP-CBY arriving at Lima Jorge Chavez Airport on November 2, 1977. It was first flown on August 10, 1959, and delivered on August 20, 1959, as N5538 (msn 1078) for Eastern Airlines. After nine years of service with Eastern Airlines, it was sold to LAP as ZP-CBY on December 15, 1968. LAP's three Lockheed L-188C Electras were used in the following destinations: Santa Cruz (Bolivia), Buenos Aires (Argentina), Montevideo (Uruguay), Sao Paulo and Rio de Janeiro and Lima (Peru). ZP-CBY was wfu and stored at Asuncion Airport in November 1988, where it remained, reportedly being in bad condition during 2016.

Left: The beautiful cockpit of LAP Lockheed L-188C ZP-CBZ at Asuncion Airport. Originally delivered to Eastern Airlines on August 28, 1959, as N5539 (msn 1080), the aircraft left the fleet in December 1968 and was bought by LAP on December 15, 1968. After 23 years of service, it was wfu at Asuncion in 1991. (Michel Anciaux)

Below: LAP Lockheed L-188C ZP-CBZ at Asuncion Airport on November 19, 1988.

New ACS Lockheed L-188C 9Q-CRR still wears the old LAP color scheme at N'Djili Airport on February 21, 1995. The aircraft was bought by ACS in the Democratic Republic of the Congo on February 18, 1994, as 9Q-CRR, but it was quickly sold to TSA in December 1994. On December 18, 1995, TSA was flying from N'Djili Airport to Angola with 144 passengers on board; the Electra was overloaded by approximately 40 passengers and crashed near Cahungula in the province of Lunda Norte in Angola. Sadly, there were no survivors. (Michel Anciaux)

Aerocondor Colombia Lockheed L-188A HK-1415 at Medellin Airport in May 1970. Delivered to American Airlines as N6120A (msn 1081) *Flagship Newark* on August 17, 1959, the aircraft was leased to the McCarthy Presidential Committee from March to July 1968 and then returned to American Airlines. It remained in this fleet until it was sold to Aerocondor Colombia as HK-1415 on April 17, 1970. It was wfu at Barranquilla Airport in Colombia in 1979 and scrapped during the 1980s. (R.M Collection)

Air California Lockheed L-188C N123US at San Francisco Airport in April 1971. Delivered to NWO on August 11, 1959, as N123US with msn 1082, this aircraft was sold to the San Diego Padres on February 17, 1969, and was later bought by Western Skyways on November 26, 1969. It was leased back to the San Diego Padres on the same day and then subsequently bought by Air California on July 21, 1970. It was re-registered as N123AC on March 8, 1976, and sold to Mandala Airlines from Indonesia in November 1979 as PK-RLD. It was wfu in 1995 and bought by Air Spray Canada on August 3, 1995, as C-FVFI. Following this, it was flown to Red Deer Airport in Alberta Canada and used for spare parts on its Lockheed L-188 fleet. It was still intact in basic Mandala livery in 2004. (R.M Collection)

Zantop International Airlines Lockheed L-188AF N282F, still in basic Overseas National Airways colors, at Willow Run Airport in August 1975. Originally delivered to National Airlines as N5006K (msn 1084) on August 30, 1959, it was bought by Pan Aero International Corporation on January 11, 1968, and leased to ONA. It was converted to L-188AF standard in July 1968 and bought by ONA on December 31, 1968. It was sold to Zantop International Airlines on October 21, 1974, and leased to Hawaiian Airlines from September 1976 to October 1977, and it was then leased to Great Northern Airlines from March to June 1978. It was eventually returned to Zantop International Airlines and was then sold to TMC Airlines in April 2000 and stored at Willow Run Airport. It was later sold to Rockland Aerospace Inc at Willow Run Airport on February 26, 2013. (R.M Collection)

Great Northern Airlines Lockheed L-188CF N402GN at Toronto Pearson Airport in January 1977. First flown on August 26, 1959, and delivered to NWO on August 30, 1959, as N124US (msn 1085), the aircraft left the NWO fleet in September 1966 and was sold to American Flyers Airline. It was then leased to several operators, including Falair, Jatco, Jet Research and American Jet Industries, and was converted to L-188CF standard in June 1975. It was leased to Fairbanks Air Service on June 16, 1975, which became Great Northern Airlines in June 1976, and was re-registered as N402GN. The aircraft was then sold to Flemming International Airways in September 1980, which became CAM Air International on September 1, 1983, and was leased to Spirit of America Airlines in December 1985. It was wfu at Greenville Spartenburg International Airport, and its registration was cancelled on February 26, 1993. (R.M Collection)

Copa Panama Lockheed L-188A N7138C still wears the old Western Airlines colors as it awaits departure at Tocumen Airport, Panama City, on December 10, 1973. It was delivered to Western Airlines as N7138C (msn 1087) on September 4, 1959, and was stored and wfu at Las Vegas Airport in 1969. It was bought by the Concare Aircraft Leasing Corporation on November 24, 1970. Leased to several airliners, including Ecuatoriana and Copa Panama from November 1973 till April 1974, the aircraft was then bought by American Jet Industries on May 31, 1974, and converted to L-188AF standard in March 1975. It was sold to Valley Trading Company in May 1975 as *El Exportador* and was later bought by Aerocondor Colombia on May 15, 1975. On July 10, 1975, N7138C suddenly veered to the right shortly after take-off from runway 12 at El Dorado Airport, sank back and crashed into an Aerocosta Douglas DC-6(F) on the cargo apron — both aircraft were destroyed by the fire.

Lockheed Corporation P-3 Orion

The Orion is a land-based, long-range, anti-submarine warfare patrol aircraft that has been in operation since the 1960s. The current model, the P-3C Update III, and the signals intelligence variant, the EP-3E 'Aries', are still in service with multiple air forces (including the United States Navy, Royal New Zealand Air Force, Royal Australian Air Force, Spanish Air Force, Royal Canadian Air Force, and Japanese Maritime Self-Defence Force) and perform missions all over the world, most recently flying from Greece to the Black Sea and the Balkans for anti-submarine warfare patrol missions near Ukraine. Although Lockheed based the P-3 on the L-188 Electra commercial airliner, the Orion is easily distinguished from the Electra by its tail stinger or MAD Boom, which is used for the magnetic detection of submarines. Numerous navies and air forces around the world continue to use the P-3, primarily for maritime patrol, reconnaissance, anti-surface warfare and anti-submarine warfare. A total of 757 P-3s have been built; early models included the P-3A and P-3B, and later the P-3C. With more than 400 aircraft flown worldwide by 21 operators in 17 countries, the P-3 remains a reliable asset in 2022.

Above: United States Department of Commerce and the National Oceanic and Atmospheric Administration Lockheed WP-3D Orion N43RF at RAF Mildenhall Air Base in November 1979. This aircraft was used to monitor oceans, weather and the environment of US territories. (R.M Collection)

Opposite above: United States Navy Lockheed VP-3A Orion 150511 (msn 5037) at Zaventem Airport, Brussels, in June 1989. (Michel Anciaux)

Opposite middle: United States Navy Lockheed NP-3C Orion 158227 (msn 5551) at Naval Air Station Moffet Field (California). This aircraft was part of the Oceanographic Research Squadron during Project *Magnet* (1951–1991). (R.M Collection)

Opposite below: United States Navy Lockheed P-3C Orion 156525 (msn 5519) at Valkenburg Naval Air Base, The Netherlands, on January 16, 1973.

Lineas Aereas de Costa Rica (LACSA) Lockheed L-188CF TI-LRO at Juan Santamaria Airport, Costa Rica, on November 10, 1980. Originally delivered to Eastern Airlines as N5540 (msn 1088) on September 17, 1959, the aircraft left the Eastern fleet in November 1968 and was sold to International Aerodyne Inc on November 14, 1968. It was bought by Falconair Sweden as SE-FGA *Sky Express* on January 15, 1969; the company ceased operations in November 1970, and the aircraft returned to International Aerodyne on February 25, 1971, as N5540. It was then sold to Voyager 1000 Travel Club on April 29, 1971, and was re-registered as N11VG on May 24, 1971. It was subsequently sold to International Air Leases on November 21, 1973, and stored at Miami Airport, being converted to L-188CF standard in 1976. It was bought by LACSA as TI-LRO on July 5, 1977, and after four years of service it was bought by Trans Union Asset Management Corporation on July 21, 1981. It was stored and wfu at Miami Airport in 1984 and scrapped during 1985.

Holiday Airlines Lockheed L-188C N971HA at San Jose Airport in June 1972. Delivered to PSA on November 6, 1959, as N171PS (msn 1091) the aircraft was bought by Friendkin Aeronautics in January 1961 and leased to PSA on January 16, 1961, and subsequently purchased by the company on February 2, 1963. It was sold to Harry A. Trueblood in August 1968 and leased to Holiday Airlines, which then bought the aircraft on November 7, 1969. Holiday Airlines had operated (through lease and purchase) this aircraft since 1965, alongside a de Havilland Dove and three other Lockheed L-188Cs, but all ceased services in November 1974. It was leased to a number of carriers, including PSA, Evergreen Int Airlines and Summit Airlines and was then bought by Channel Express as G-CEXS in October 1990. It was sold in March 2003 to Air Spray Canada as C-GZCF and was still active in 2022. (R.M Collection)

National Airlines Lockheed L-188A N5008K at Philadelphia International Airport in September 1964. It was delivered to National Airlines as N5008K on September 24, 1959, and left the fleet in December 1968. It was bought by Pan Aero International Corporation on December 30, 1968, and was wfu at Miami Airport in January 1969. The aircraft was then sold to Byron F. Sherrill on June 28, 1973, and later bought by California Airmotive Corporation on July 30, 1973. It was sold to American Jet Industries on May 31, 1974, converted to L-188CF standard in February 1975 and bought by Flemming International Airways (CAM Air International) as N666F on February 21, 1975. It was wfu at Miami Airport Florida in 1988 and broken up in 1990. (R.M Collection)

Varig Lockheed L-188A PP-VLC, flying from Rio de Janeiro Santos Dumont Airport to São Paulo Congonhas Airport on October 24, 1988. Originally delivered to American Airlines as N6122A (msn 1093) *Flagship Albany* on September 23, 1959, the aircraft left the fleet in April 1970 and was sold to Varig as PP-VLC on April 6, 1970. It was leased to Cruzeiro do Sul between March and June 1975, and, when it returned to Varig, it was stored at São Paulo Airport in January 1993. It was bought by Blue Airlines in August 1993 as 9Q-CDL.

Left and above: Varig Lockheed L-188A PP-VLC at São Paulo Congonhas Airport on October 24, 1988.

Below: Lockheed L-188A PP-VLC and PP-VLX at São Paulo Congonhas Airport on October 24, 1988.

Lockheed L-188A Blue Airlines 9Q-CDL (msn 1093) takes off at N'Djili Airport, still in the colors of Varig, on November 2, 1994. It was wfu at N'Djili Airport in November 1995 and was broken up in 1996. (Michel Anciaux)

Western Airlines Lockheed L-188A N7139C at Las Vegas Airport in May 1969. This aircraft was delivered to Western Airlines on September 26, 1959, as N7139C (msn 1094). It was wfu and stored at Las Vegas Airport Nevada during 1968. It was then converted to L-188PF standard and bought by International Jet Air as CF-IJY *Yukon Lady* on March 30, 1971. It was sold to Allarco Development Ltd in November 1976 as N7139C and leased to Great Northern Airlines on June 1, 1977. It was returned to Allarco on January 26, 1978, and re-registered on April 20, 1978, as N405GN. The aircraft was sold to Flemming International Airways (CAM Air International) on November 20, 1980. (R.M Collection)

CAM Air International Lockheed L-188PF N405GN *Diane Jennever* at Miami Airport in December 1983. The aircraft was bought by Integrity Aircraft Sales Inc, and was subsequently wfu and stored at Greenville-Spartanburg International Airport in South Carolina in October 1989. (R.M Collection)

LANSA Lockheed L-188A OB-R-945 at Jorge Chávez Airport on November 12, 1971. Originally delivered to Braniff Airways on October 1, 1959, as N9706C (msn 1095), this aircraft was bought by Crocker Citizens National Bank on March 28, 1968, and leased to Braniff the same day. It was returned to Crocker Citizens Bank on March 27, 1969, and subsequently sold to Boeing on October 9, 1970, after which it was wfu and stored at Wichita Airport in Kansas. It was bought by LANSA on January 26, 1971, as OB-R-945 *Juan Santos Atahualpa* and stored at Lima Airport in December 1971. LANSA began acquiring ex-Braniff Electras in December 1969 for use on its domestic routes. The Lockheed L-188's good high-altitude performance was particularly suited to these routes, many of these mountain airports being comfortably above 5000ft. LANSA had a fleet of four Electras, but unfortunately two of them crashed: OB-R-941 (msn 1086) at Puerto Inca on December 24, 1971, and OB-R-939 (msn 1106) at Cuzco on August 9, 1970. The operating certificate was cancelled for all LANSA Electras in December 1971, and the two remaining Electras, OB-R-945 and OB-R-946, were sold. (Ad Jan Altevogt Collection)

Century 2000 Travel Club Lockheed L-188A N5009K at Miami Airport in March 1972. Delivered to National Airlines on October 5, 1969, as N5009K (msn 1096), this aircraft was bought by Pan Aero International on December 30, 1968, and leased to Century 2000 Travel Club in May 1971. It was also leased to Trans Artic Airlines and Astroair Service before being converted to L-188C standard in October 1972 and subsequently leased to Air Manila International as PI-C1063 on August 24, 1973. It was bought by International Air Leases Inc on December 17, 1973, and leased to Air Manila, later being re-registered as RP-C1063 in November 1974 and bought by Dolphin Aviation on June 12, 1975, before being leased again to Air Manila. American Jet Industries bought the aircraft on July 10, 1978, and it was converted to L-188CF standard in October 1979. It was sold to Iscargo Iceland on December 24, 1979, as TF-ISC and was later bought by Eagle Air Iceland on March 11, 1982, being re-registered as TF-VLN on March 12, 1983. (R.M Collection)

Iscargo Iceland Lockheed L-188CF TF-ISC at Rotterdam Zestienhoven Airport in June 10, 1980. Sold to Eagle Air Iceland on March 11, 1982, and re-registered on March 12, 1983, this aircraft was bought by Fleming International Airways as N4465F on September 17, 1983. It was then bought by JBQ Aviation Corporation on March 31, 1989. On July 14, 1990, on a flight from Aruba Airport to Panama City, the L-188CF's number 3 propeller failed and broke apart, striking the number 4 propeller, which also separated and then crossed underneath the aircraft, slicing through the fuselage, cables, hydraulics and pressure vessel, and damaging the number 2 engine. Number 2, 3 and 4 engines were shut down, and an emergency landing was carried out at Aruba Airport with no brakes, 10 degree flaps and limited flight controls on. All three crew survived, but the aircraft was written off.

Eagle Air Iceland Lockheed L-188CF TF-VLN at Amsterdam Schiphol Airport in September 1983. (Peter de Groot)

Voyager 1000 Travel Club Lockheed L-188C N12VG at Indianapolis International Airport in August 1972. Delivered to Eastern Airlines on October 14, 1959, as N5541 (msn 1098), this aircraft was bought by International Aerodyne on October 11, 1968, and sold to Falconair Sweden as SE-FGB on December 20, 1968, but the company ceased operations in November 1970. It was bought by Voyager 1000 Travel Club from Indianapolis (Indiana) on April 29, 1971, as N12VG, however this company declared bankruptcy and ceased operations on May 1, 1972. The aircraft was then bought by International Air leases Inc on April 21, 1973, and was re-registered as N5541B on March 17, 1975. It was converted to L-188CF standard in May 1976 and leased to Carib West Airways from June 1976 to March 1978. It was bought by Hawaiian Airlines as N345HA in July 1978 and sold to Zantop International Airlines on September 2, 1980. It was eventually bought by Fred Olsen as LN-FOO on June 14, 1994, in full DHL standard livery. It was sold to Aviation Services Inc on November 24, 1999, as N590HG and stored at Opa Locka Airport in April 2007. (R.M Collection)

Carib West Airways Lockheed L-188CF N5541B leaves Port of Spain Piarco International Airport, Trinidad, on October 18, 1977. Carib West Airways was formed on March 18, 1971, by private US and Barbadian parties and began charter operations in the same month with two Douglas DC-3s from Barbados Grantley Adams International Airport. Two Convair CV-340s were then leased, with the L-188CF from International Air Leases following soon after for cargo flights to Miami, Jamaica, Trinidad and Puerto Rico from Barbados. The company ceased operations in 1979.

ALM Antillean Airlines Cargo Lockheed L-188AF N665F at Miami Airport on November 26, 1992. Originally delivered to American Airlines as N6123A (msn 1100) on October 22, 1959, this aircraft was in service till January 1967, being bought by Air California on January 3, 1967, as N289AC and sold to GATX Booth Aircraft Company on December 18, 1968. It was leased again to Air California before being sold F. B. Ayer & Associates on November 7, 1969, and stored at Fort Worth in Texas in 1970. It was then converted to L-188AF standard in August 1977. It has since been owned by a number of leasing companies and flown by many airlines, including Flemming International, CAM Air International, Spirit of America Airlines, TPI Int Airways, ALM, and Air Atlantique (renamed as Atlantic Cargo) in June 1995 as G-LOFC, and Atlantic Airlines in June 2004. The aircraft was bought by Buffalo Airways, based at Hay River, Northwest Territories, on May 14, 2013, as C-GXFC and is still active in 2022. (R.M Collection)

Buffalo Airways Lockheed L-188AF C-GXF (msn 1100) arriving at Vancouver International Airport (British Columbia) on November 21, 2021. (André Klöckne)

Shillelaghs Travel Club Lockheed L-188C N125US at Tucson Airport Arizona in October 1981. Delivered to NWO as N125US (msn 1101), this aircraft was sold to American Flyers on November 14, 1966, and leased to Dominicana from October 31, 1970 to April 30, 1971. After this, it was bought by California Airmotive Corporation on May 13, 1971, and sold to the Shillelaghs Travel Club on January 17, 1972. Popularly known as the Emerald Shillelaghs Chowder and Marching Society from Fairfax in Virginia, this travel club operated a single Lockheed L-188C to tourist destinations both within the US and overseas from 1972 to 1986. The aircraft was sold to JBQ Aviation Airways in March 1986 and converted to L-188CF standard in June 1986. It was then leased to TPI International Airways in August 1986 and was flown to Miami Airport in April 1989, being broken up in December of the same year. (R.M Collection)

Argentine Navy Lockheed L-188PF 5-T-1 at Buenos Aires Ezeiza Airport on October 28, 1988. Delivered to American Airlines as N6124A (msn 1102) on October 23, 1959, this aircraft was in service with American Airlines till June 1970, after which it was bought by Oklahoma Airmotive. It was sold to McCulloch Airmotive in February 1971 and was transferred to McCulloch International Airlines on May 10, 1972. It was then bought by the Argentine Navy in December 1973 as 5-T-1 and converted to L-188PF standard in February 1974. It was wfu at Trelew Naval Air Base on August 31, 2009.

Century 2000 Travel Club Lockheed L-188C N126US at Miami Airport, June 16, 1972. Delivered to NWO on November 14, 1959, as N126US (msn 1105) this aircraft left service with NWO and was sold to Flyers Airline on January 23, 1967. It was then bought by Aircraft Lessors Inc on June 15, 1971, and leased to Aeroclub International on the same date. Following this, it was leased to Century 2000 Travel Club in February 1972 and returned in May 1973, after which it was bought by MCA Leasing Corporation on September 12, 1973, and converted to L-188CF standard at that time. It was leased to several Latin American operators, including Aerocosta Colombia, Guyana Airways and APSA Costa Rica, before being returned in March 1977. It was leased again, this time to the Cooperativa Nacional de Montecillos from Costa Rica in May 1977. On June 30, 1977, the L-188CF was flying from San Jose Juan Santamaria Airport to Caracas when the Electra went missing over the Caribbean Sea near Bocas del Toro (Panama) with four crew members on board. The Electra was transporting 16,330kg of frozen meat when radio contact was lost; a search and rescue mission covering over 1,417 square nautical miles was conducted but failed to find the Electra. (Peter de Groot)

Air Florida Lockheed L-188C N25AF *City of Jacksonville* at Miami Airport on May 29, 1975. This aircraft was delivered to Northwest west Airlines as N128US (msn 1111) on December 10, 1959. It was bought by Pierce Leasing Corporation on November 3, 1971, and leased to Muskie Travel Committee from April 18, 1972 until July 1972 and was then sold to Air Holiday in the same month. It was bought by Jet Leasing Inc on May 26, 1973, and leased to Air Florida on August 1, 1974, later being bought by the company in June 1975. It was sold to American Jet Industries in July 1977 and bought by Nordair Canada as C-GNDZ on February 8, 1978. (R.M Collection)

Nordair Lockheed L-188C C-GNDZ at Montreal Dorval Airport on April 20, 1986. Nordair Canada purchased two Electras for use on a contract given by the Canadian government for iceberg reconnaissance activities in the Atlantic shipping lanes. Both Electras were very extensively modified by Canadair Ltd to use surface radar, thermal sensors, visual observation systems and other facilities. Nordair merged with Canadian Pacific Airlines on April 26, 1987. The aircraft was sold to Aeriennes Inter Quebec on September 5, 1989, and a few months later it was bought by Aerobureau Corporation in February 1990. It was sold to Intair on September 3, 1991, and bought by New ACS in April 1992 as 9Q-CRY. (Pierre Langlois)

New ACS Lockheed L-188C 9Q-CRY at N'Djili Airport on March 15, 1993. This aircraft (msn 1111) was delivered in April 1992, but it was damaged beyond repair at an unknown location in August 1992 in the Democratic Republic of the Congo. No further information is available about the location or the accident. (Michel Anciaux)

Omni Aircraft Sales Inc Lockheed L-188C N8LG at Amsterdam Schiphol Airport in April 1979. First flown on November 25, 1959, and delivered to NWO on December 15, 1959, as N129US with (msn 1112), this aircraft was sold to International Skyways Inc on January 20, 1970, and was re-registered as N777DP on April 22, 1970. It was then bought by Pignatari SA from Brazil as PT-DZK on October 4, 1971, and later purchased by Omni Aircraft Sales on February 24, 1976, as N8LG. After this, the aircraft was bought by the National Leasing Corporation in September 1981. The next buyer was TPI International Airways in April 1985, which converted the aircraft to L-188CF standard in July 1985, and re-registered it as N360Q on July 18, 1985. It was then leased to Air Bridge Carriers on June 1, 1989, and re-registered as N360WS on November 12, 1989. It was chartered to World Airline Gambia from April 8, 1990 to January 17, 1992, and was then bought by JBQ Aviation on April 8, 1992, after which it was re-registered as N360Q in December 1992. While in this fleet, it was leased to several airlines, including Renown Aviation, Hunting Cargo and Channel Express. It was stored in October 2000 and bought by Air Spray as C-GYVI on January 23, 2003, only to be stored again, this time at Red Deer Airport in 2007.

Channel Express Lockheed L-188CF N360Q at Belfast International Airport in June 1998. (R.M Collection)

LANSA Lockheed L-188A N9709C at Tucson Airport Arizona on June 24, 1972. Delivered to Braniff Airways on January 9, 1960, as N9709C (msn 1114), this aircraft was bought by Crocker Citizens National Bank on March 28, 1968, and leased back to Braniff Airways till March 1969. It was then sold to F.B Ayer & Associates on July 10, 1970, and bought by Boeing on February 10, 1971. After this, it was sold to LANSA as OB-R-946 on April 30, 1971, and returned to Boeing on May 7, 1971, after LANSA's operational certificate was cancelled because of two Electra crashes. Boeing sold the aircraft back to F.B Ayer & Associates Inc on July 3, 1974, and the next day it was bought by Holiday Airlines and was re-registered as N972HA on September 18, 1974. It was then sold to Air California as N124AC on April 22, 1975, but the registration was cancelled in January 1980 and the aircraft exported to Indonesia for Mandala Airlines as PK-RLE. The aircraft was wfu and stored at Jakarta Airport Halim Airport in Indonesia in October 1986, and it was broken up by October 1997. (Peter de Groot)

McCulloch International Airlines Lockheed L-188A N6126A at Long Beach Airport California in May 1972. This aircraft was originally delivered to American Airlines as N6126A (msn 1116) on January 13, 1960. After 10 years, it was bought by McCulloch Properties on March 30, 1970, and transferred to McCulloch International Airlines on May 10, 1972, later returning on October 30, 1975. It was sold to FGH Financial Corporation on October 30, 1975, and was subsequently leased back to McCulloch International Airlines on the same day. It was bought by American Jet Industries on March 15, 1977, and converted to L-188AF standard in July 1977, being bought by Great Northern Airlines on July 29, 1977. (R.M Collection)

Great Northern Airlines Lockheed L-188AF N404GN at Willow Run Airport Michigan in October 1977. Previously registered as N6126A, it was re-registered as N404GN on September 29, 1977. This aircraft was sold to Flemming International Airways (CAM Air International) on September 15, 1980, and was re-registered as N669F on November 22, 1980. It was bought by First Security Bank of Utah on November 11, 1988, and leased to TPI International Airways/ Air Bridge Carriers until June 1991. Bought by Fred Olsen Air Transport in June 1991 as LN-FOL, it was painted with EMS titles in June 1992, and in February 1993 it was liveried in full DHL colors with a Fred Olsen logo on the tail. It was stored at Coventry Airport, UK, in August 1997 and re-registered as G-LOFG on June 21, 2004, but the registration was cancelled in the same month. It was later used as a fire trainer and was broken up in 2011. (R.M Collection)

Great Northern Alaska International Lockheed L-188AF N669F at Atlanta Airport in May 1981.

Argentine Navy Lockheed L-188PF 5-T-2 at Naval Air Station Pensacola, Florida, in 1982. Delivered to American Airlines on February 3, 1960, as N6129A (msn 1120) *Flagship San Diego*, the aircraft was bought by McCulloch Properties Inc on April 29, 1970, and transferred to McCulloch International Airlines on May 10, 1972. It was sold to the Argentine Navy as 5-T-2 *Ushuaia* on December 20, 1973, and was converted to L-188PF standard in March 1974. The aircraft became 6-P-106 in September 1995, and has been preserved since 2006 in the Bahia Blanca Naval Aviation Museum.

Argentine Navy Lockheed L-188PF 5-T-3 *Rio Grande* at Rio Gallegos Airport on November 4, 1988. Originally delivered to American Airlines on February 17, 1960, as N6131A (msn 1122) *Flagship Little Rock*, the aircraft left the fleet after nine years of service and was bought by McCulloch Properties Inc on May 30, 1969, after which it was transferred to McCulloch International Airlines on May 10, 1972. Next, it was sold to the Argentine Navy and delivered on December 27, 1973, as 0693/5-T-3 *Rio Grande*. It was converted to L-188PF standard in March 1974, decommissioned in 1995, stored at Buenos Aires Ezeiza Airport, bought by a private buyer in 1997, and has been preserved since 2008 in the town of 9 de Abril, Esteban, in the province of Buenos Aires.

Varig Lockheed L-188A PP-VJW at Rio de Janeiro Santos Dumont Airport on November 10, 1973. Delivered to American Airlines on February 24, 1960, as N6133A (msn 1124) *Flagship Baltimore*, this aircraft was sold to Varig on March 15, 1968, as PP-VJW. Although Varig was not an original Electra customer, its predecessor REAL had intended to purchase three Electras from American Airlines' large fleet. After the REAL/Varig merger had taken place, Varig picked up REAL's Electra order and accepted the L-188As from American Airlines. These three were quickly followed by others, as the Electra proved itself over Varig's huge domestic network. Other Electras were gradually acquired in the late 1960s, and two of the passenger/cargo convertibles were bought in January 1970. Even though the Electras have been used on some international routes, they continue to serve as the backbone of the domestic routes, and several Electras have been leased to Cruzeiro/Trans Brasil in a pooling arrangement for the operation of some very high-density routes, including between Santos Dumont Airport to São Paulo Congonhas Airport.

Interlink Airlines Pty Lockheed L-188A HR-AMM at Lanseria Airport on March 11, 1996. This aircraft was bought from Varig as PP-VJW, which had been wfu at Sao Paulo in 1992. It was then bought by Interlink Airlines Pty in October 1993 as HR-AMM and was wfu at Lanseria Airport in South Africa in February 1996. Later, it was sold to Air Spray at Red Deer Airport in August 2008 as C-GZYH, but the registration was cancelled in February 2012, and the aircraft was broken up. (Michel Anciaux)

Lloyd Aereo Boliviano Lockheed L-188A CP-853 at Buenos Aires Ezeiza Airport on December 2, 1968. Originally delivered to American Airlines as N6134A (msn 1125) *Flagship Memphis*. After eight years of service with American Airlines, it was bought by Lloyd Aereo Boliviano as CP-853 on August 12, 1968, to replace its old piston equipment for its few foreign routes to Santiago de Chile, Lima, Buenos Aires, Argentina, Asuncion and São Paulo. It was sold to TAM Transporte Aéreo de Militar Bolivia as TAM-69 in 1973. (R.M Collection)

TAM Transporte Aéreo Militar Bolivia Lockheed L-188A TAM-01 at Miami Airport in July 1978. This aircraft was re-registered from TAM-69 to TAM-01 in May 1975, and it was seen derelict at La Paz El Alto Airport in the 1980s. Luckily, in 2015, it was saved by the Bolivian Aeronautical Museum at La Paz El Alto. (R.M Collection)

TSA Lockheed L-188A 9Q-CCV at N'Djili Airport on November 23, 1994. This aircraft was delivered to American Airlines as N6135A (msn 1126) on March 21,1960. Bought by Varig as PP-VJV on December 30, 1967, it was subsequently sold to New ACS in November 1992 as 9Q-CRS, then bought by TSA in October 1993 as 9Q-CCV. It was written off when the nose gear collapsed during a landing at N'Djili Airport on January 21, 1994. (Michel Anciaux)

Inair Panama Lockheed L-188PF HP-684 at Miami Airport on May 29, 1977. Delivered to Western Airlines on May 17, 1961, as N7142C (msn 1128), this aircraft was converted to L-188PF standard in December 1968. It was leased to Pacific Western Airlines as CF-ZST on March 3, 1971, and soon after bought by International Jetair Ltd on April 16, 1971. After the sale, it continued to be leased to Pacific Western Airlines until it was sold to MCA Leasing Corporation on April 13, 1976, as N417MA. It was leased to Inair Panama from June 1976 to October 1976, and was bought by that company on October 5, 1976, as HP-684. It was sold to Shackleton Aviation in September 1977 and later leased to Aeronaves del Peru as OB-R1138. (R.M Collection)

Aeronaves del Peru Lockheed L-188PF OB-R-1138 at Miami Airport on October 15, 1977. This aircraft was leased from Shackleton Aviation and returned in February 1978 as N417MA, later being bought by Hawaiian Airlines on February 14, 1978 and sold to United States Lease Financing Inc on July 26, 1978. It was leased back to Hawaiian Airlines on the same date, as N342HA and returned to the US Lease Financing Inc in August 1980. After being leased to Zantop International Airlines on September 2, 1980, that company bought the aircraft in April 1985, selling it to Fred Olsen Air Transport in May 1994 as LN-FON for cargo flights. It was bought by Atlantic Airlines in May 2000 as G-LOFF for spare parts for the company's fleet, and it was broken up on February 13, 2008, at Coventry Airport.

Northwest Territorial Lockheed L-188AF C-FIJV at Vancouver Airport in August 1981. Delivered to Western Airlines as N7143C (msn 1129) on May 24, 1961, it was converted to L-188AF standard in March 1969 and bought by International Jetair Ltd in March 1971. In 1976, the company merged with Northwest Territorial Airways. Company merged with Northwest Territorial Airways in 1976. Northwest Territorial operated both scheduled and charter cargo and passenger services in Northern Canada in support of oil and mineral operations. The aircraft was sold to Air Bridge Carriers in March 1991 and was re-registered as G-FIJV in August of that year. (R.M Collection)

Hunting Cargo Airlines Lockheed L-188AF G-FIJV at Brussel Zaventem Airport on March 11, 1995. The aircraft was bought by Hunting Cargo Airlines on August 15, 1992, and was re-registered as EI-HCE in April 1997 and wfu in June 1998. It was bought by Atlantic Airlines as G-FIJV on September 14, 1998, and then later wfu at Coventry Airport in January 2007. The aircraft was broken up in May 2013, and the registration was finally cancelled on September 29, 2016.

National Center for Atmospheric Research Lockheed L-188C N308D at Atlanta Airport, Georgia, in May 1975. This aircraft was initially bought by Capital Airlines, but it was not taken up and was instead leased to the US Navy from July 1960 to January 1961. It was then sold to PSA on January 26, 1961, as N175PS (msn 1130) before being sold to Gelco Leasing Company on February 29, 1968, as N595KR. The next day, this aircraft was leased to King Resources Company. On May 15, 1972, the aircraft was bought by Omni Aircraft sales Inc and on May 18, 1973, it was leased to the National Center for Atmospheric Research and subsequently bought by the center on December 1, 1975, as N308D. It was sold to the National Science Foundation on January 13, 1976, and transferred back to National Center for Atmospheric Research on the same day. It was wfu at Davis Monthan Air Force Base (AFB) in August 2001 and subsequently bought by Neptune Aviation Service in May 2003. It was exported to Air Spray Canada as C-FLXT in December 2006 and was still active in 2022.

TAN Lockheed L-188C HR-TNL at Tegucigalpa Toncontín Airport in September 1970. Ordered by Capital Airlines but not taken up, this aircraft was delivered to Braniff Airways as N9710C (msn 1134) on May 10, 1962. The aircraft was purchased by Crocker Citizens National Bank on March 28, 1968, and leased back to Braniff Airways until March 27, 1969, before being sold to Boeing on April 28, 1969, which then sold it to F.B Ayer & Associates in May 1969. It was bought by TAN as HR-TNL in August 1969 and converted to L-188CF standard in July 1976. During a cargo flight from San Pedro Sula Airport in Honduras to Tegucigalpa Toncontin Airport on March 21, 1990, HR-TNL approached Toncontin Airport runway 01 in very poor weather. The crew failed to realize that the Electra's altitude was too low and crashed into southern slopes of the Cerro Hula at 2500ft below the 7000ft minimum safe altitude point. The Electra was destroyed, and all three crew members were killed. (R.M Collection)

TAN Lockheed L-188 HR-TNN at San Pedro Sula Airport on November 1, 1980, wearing a new color scheme. TAN was founded in 1947, and in 1950 the company started scheduled passenger and cargo services. In November 1, 1991, the company merged with another Honduran airline, SAHSA.

American Flyers Airlines (AFA) Lockheed L-188C N182H taxies for take off at Amsterdam Schiphol Airport on June 19, 1966. This aircraft was bought by AFA as N182H (msn 1135) on January 17, 1963. AFA was the first non-scheduled carrier to purchase an Electra, and it was very satisfied with its purchase, immediately adding four more aircraft to its fleet. This Electra has been operated by a considerable number of airlines, including Blue Grass Ventures, ONA, Ports of Call Travel Club, Gulf Air Transport, Air Traffic Service Corporation, Northwest Territorial Airways, JBQ Aviation and TPI International Airways. It was converted to L-188CF standard in September 1985, wfu at Opa Locka Airport Florida in December 1995 and broken up in 1996. (Adjan Altevogt)

Varig Lockheed L-188C PP-VLB at Sao Paulo Congonhas Airport on October 24, 1988. This aircraft was delivered to NWO on March 14, 1961, as N133US (msn 1137) and was converted to L-188PF standard in 1969. After nine years of service with NWO it left the fleet after being bought by Varig as PP-VLB on June 3, 1970. The Electra was used for passenger and cargo flights, and it was stored at Porto Alegre in Brazil in January 1992. In November 1993, Filair bought the Electra as 9Q-CUU.

Filair Lockheed L-188PF 9Q-CUU N'Djili Airport on January 14, 1995. Filair is an airline based in the Democratic Republic of the Congo, and it mainly operates out of N'Djili Airport; it was founded in 1987 and ceased operations in 2015. The company used a large fleet of different types of aircraft, including Douglas DC-6s, DC-7s, Lockheed L-188s, Vickers Viscounts, Convair 580s, Boeing 707s and Antonov AN24s, 26s and 32s. (Michel Anciaux)

Air Bridge Lockheed L-188PF C-FIJR at Zaventem Airport in December 1990. Originally delivered to NWO on March 29, 1961, as N134US (msn 1138), it was converted to L-188PF standard in April 1968 and purchased by International Jetair Ltd on January 19, 1971, as CF-IJR. It was then leased to Imperial Oil Ltd in 1972 and sold to Northwest Territorial Airways in 1983. It was bought by Air Bridge in December 1990 – which was renamed Hunting Cargo Airlines on August 15, 1992 – and sold to Atlantic Cargo on November 21, 1997 – which was renamed Atlantic Airlines in January 1998. This aircraft was bought by Conair Group on October 8, 2010, as C-GYCG, before being sold to Buffalo Airways on October 31, 2016. It was stored and wfu at Abbotsford Airport, Canada. (R.M Collection)

Varig Lockheed L-188CF PP-VLA at Rio de Janeiro Galeão Airport on November 13, 1973. This aircraft was delivered to NWO on April 7, 1961, as N135US (msn 1139), and it was converted to L-188PF standard in 1969 and bought by Varig on June 2, 1970, as PP-VLA. Due to its success among passengers, Varig acquired more Electras, two in 1967 (PP-VJU and PP-VJV) and one in 1968 (PP-VJW), totalling 11 Electras in the fleet. PP-VLA and PP-VLB were convertible, meaning they could be configured for cargo or passenger needs, and these two Electras operated cargo flights for a short time, especially to Manaus, but were soon converted to passenger-only duties. The Varig Electra was also famous for its lounge at the end of the passengers' cabin, which had seven VIP seats. In 1975, the Varig Electras started working the air shuttle between Rio and São Paulo, and in November 1976 the company acquired two more Electras (PP-VNJ and PP-VNK), meaning there was a total of 13 Electras operating the shuttle flight between Dumont Airport and São Paulo Congonhas Airport. The flights only took 50 minutes and were operated every 15 minutes on weekdays and every 30 minutes on weekends and holidays. The flights with the Lockheed L-188As came to an end in November 1991. One Electra, PP-VJM, was saved by the Campos dos Afonsos Aerospace Museum, near Rio de Janeiro. PP-VLA was stored at Porto Alegre Airport in January 1992 and bought by Filair as 9Q-CVK in November 1993, which re-registered it as 9Q-CGD in December 1993. In July 1994, the Electra was damaged beyond repair somewhere in Angola, but no details are available.

This Varig Electra, PP-VLC, is flying from Rio de Janeiro Santos Dumont Airport to São Paulo Congonhas Airport on October 24, 1988, just crossing the famous Sugarloaf mountain (1,299ft). On the far left you can see is Copacabana Beach.

A line up of three Varig Electras at São Paulo Congonhas Airport on October 24, 1988.

A look at the four big Allison 501-D13 turboprops of a Varig Electra. Sao Paulo Congonhas Airport, October 24, 1988.

Reeve Aleutian Airways Lockheed L-188PF N9744C at Anchorage Airport, Alaska. Delivered to Western Airlines on February 3, 1961, as N9744C (msn 1140), this aircraft was converted to L-188PF standard in December 1968 and sold to Reeve Aleutian Airways on September 26, 1970. Registration was cancelled on August 28, 2002, and the aircraft was bought by Atlantic Airlines as G-LOFH. It was re-registered as N4HG on February 19, 2003, for Electra Aero, and then bought by Electra Airways on July 26, 2004. The aircraft was wfu at Coventry Airport. Before being bought and re-registered as C-FIJV by Buffalo Airways Ltd on May 27, 2011. C-FIJV was stored and wfu at Yellowknife Airport, Northwest Territories.

Nordic Air A.S Lockheed L-188AF LN-MOD at Frankfurt Airport in April 1973. Originally delivered to Western Airlines as N9745C (msn 1143) on February 15, 1961, the aircraft was converted to L-188AF standard in 1969. It was bought by International Jetair Ltd on March 30, 1971, as CF-IJC. Jetair ceased operations and the aircraft returned to Western Airlines as N9745C on August 17, 1971. In December of the same year, the aircraft was stored at Las Vegas Airport until August 17, 1972, when it was bought by Nordic Air as LN-MOD to be operated for SAS cargo flights. The Electra was bought by Fred Olsen A/S in November 1973 as LN-FOG, and after 24 years of service it was bought by Atlantic Cargo as G-LOFD on May 1, 1997. It was sold to Conair Aviation as C-FYYJ on February 12, 2010, and was wfu and stored at Abbotsford International Airport, Canada, on August 26, 2020.

Air to Air Lockheed L-188AF LN-FOG, flying from Copenhagen Airport to Zaventem Airport on July 27, 1985.

DHL Lockheed L-188AF LN-FOG on the Amsterdam Schiphol Airport cargo ramp with another Fred Olsen Air Transport Lockheed L-188 Electra on September 15, 1993. (R.M Collection)

Conair Aerial Firefighting Lockheed L-188(AT) C-FYYJ at Campbell River in British Columbia on September 3, 2015. This aircraft was wfu and stored at Abbotsford International Airport on August 26, 2020. (John Olafson)

Spirit of America Lockheed L-188AF N668F at Tucson Airport, Arizona, on October 31, 1989. Delivered to NWO on June 23, 1961, as N138US (msn 1144), the aircraft left the fleet after ten years of service and was bought by FPE Travel Club on September 15, 1971. It was leased to Aeronauts International in March 1972 and later sold to Jet Leasing Inc on March 15, 1972. It was leased to Air Florida on the same date and was re-registered as N24AF on February 1, 1974. It was purchased by Air Florida in August 1974 and was wfu and stored at Miami Airport in Florida in October 1976. American Jet Industries purchased the aircraft in March 1977 and converted it to L-188CF standard in July 1977. Flemming International Airways (CAM Air International) bought the Electra as N668F in November 1977, and it was wfu and stored at Tucson Airport in October 1989. Next the aircraft was bought by JBQ Aviation in December 1990, then leased to Hunting Cargo Airlines on July 24, 1992, and subsequently sold to Hunting Cargo Airlines on April 27, 1998, which leased it to Atlantic Cargo on September 14, 1998, as EI-CET. It was re-registered as G-LOFE on January 5, 1999, for Atlantic Airlines and was purchased by Buffalo Airways as C-GZFE on April 16, 2013.

Spirit of America N668F and N665F, and Aerobureau N667F line up at Tucson Airport on October 31, 1989.

TACA International Airlines Lockheed L-188AF YS-06C at Panama Tocumen Airport in March 1979. Originally delivered to TAA on August 25, 1960, as VH-TLC (msn 1147), this aircraft was stored at Melbourne Airport, Australia, in October 1970 and was later bought by the Concare Aircraft Leasing Corporation on June 6, 1972, as N188LC. It was leased to Continental Airlines from December 1, 1972, until May 1, 1973, and was then bought by the California Airmotive Corporation on December 20, 1973. It was converted to L-188AF standard in April 1975 and was purchased by TACA International Airlines as YS-06C in May 1976. TACA operated two Lockheed L-188AFs — YS-06C and YS-07C. YS-06C wa sold to Galaxy Airlines in September 1985 as N188LC and was then bought by Aero Transport in December 1988.

Lockheed L-188AF OB-1328 at Lima Jorge Chávez Airport on December 21, 1989. Bought by Aero Transporte SA Cargo as OB-1328 in December 1988, the aircraft was leased to Linhas Aéreas de Moçambique from March 20, 1989 until November 1989. It was then bought by LAMA Colombia as HK-3642X in August 1991 and re-registered to APEL Express in February 1992 as HK-3706. Next it was re-registered to Transapel as HK-3706X in March 1996 and was bought in October 2001 by Mex-Jet S.A in as XA-AEG. On March 29, 2007, during a start up at Panama Tocumen Airport for a flight to La Aurora Airport, one of the propellers of XA-AEG hit a ground power unit. The number 2 propeller disintegrated, with debris puncturing the fuselage; it was damaged beyond repair and was seen derelict at Panama Tocumen Airport by 2019. (R.M Collection)

Lynden Air Cargo Lockheed L-188AF N287F at Anchorage Airport in March 1996. Delivered to National Airlines on January 9, 1961, as N5014K (msn 1148), it was bought by Pan AeroInternational Corporation on April 4, 1968, and sold to ONA Leasing Inc in the same month. It was re-registered as N287F and was converted to L-188AF standard in October 1968. The aircraft was sold to Aero Uranus Inc on October 29, 1974, subsequently transferring to Zantop International Airlines on October 29, 1974. Next, it was re-registered to Lynden Air Cargo in May 1997 as N287F, and in October 2000 it was purchased by Air Spray Canada for spare parts. On September 13, 2001, the aircraft was wfu at Abbotsford Airport and the registration cancelled. (R.M Collection)

Ecuatoriana Lockheed L-188C HC-AVX at Miami Airport on November 7, 1971. Four Electras, three belonging to Ecuatoriana and one to ONA, wait for maintenance. This aircraft was originally delivered to Qantas on October 30, 1959, as VH-ECA (msn 2002) *Pacific Electra*, and it was sold to Air California as N359AC on June 7, 1967. Next it was purchased by F. B. Ayer & Associates on November 7, 1969, and was wfu at Forth Worth Airport, Texas. It was leased to Ecuatoriana as HC-AVX from September 7, 1971, until March 6, 1972. MCA Leasing bought the Electra in October 1975 and converted it to L-188CF standard in March 1976 before selling it to LACSA as TI-LRM in April 1976.

LACSA Carguero Lockheed L-188CF TI-LRM at Juan Santamaria Airport, Costa Rica, in February 1979. The aircraft was in service from April 1976 to August 1981 and was bought by the FBA Corporation in August 1981. It was sold to Qualley International Corporation in December 1983, leased to TPI International in February 1984, and sold to JBQ Aviation in February 1985. Next it was leased to TPI International Corporation, re-registered as N359Q in May 1985, and then leased to Servicios de Transportes Aereos Fueguinos (STAF), Argentina, in November 1986 as F-OGST. STAF was founded in 1985 in Ushuaia in order to develop cargo transportation services from Ushuaia (via Buenos Aires) to Manaus, Curacao and Miami.

STAF Lockheed L-188CF F-OGST at Miami Airport Florida on December 5, 1987. Bought from TPI International Airways in February 1987, STAF leased this aircraft to Air Bridge Carriers in October 1990 till October 1992. It was re-registered as N359Q for JBQ Aviation, and then sold to Atlantic Cargo Airlines in November 1993 as G-LOFA. It was wfu in May 1998 and broken up at Coventry Airport.

KLM Royal Dutch Airlines Lockheed L-188C PH-LLB arriving at the Amsterdam Schiphol Airport in August 1963. This aircraft was delivered to KLM on October 10, 1959, as PH-LLB (msn 2003) *Venus*. The only European operator to order the Electra was KLM, which ordered 12. The PH-LLB left KLM after nine years of service and was bought by Universal Airlines as N852U on July 21, 1968, which converted it to L-188CF standard in November 1986. First National City Bank repossessed the aircraft on May 4, 1972, and leased it to Saturn Airways on May 5, 1972. On June 27, 1974, the aircraft was purchased by Saturn.

Saturn Airways Lockheed L-188CF N852U at Oakland Airport in November 1976. Saturn Airways merged with Trans International Airlines in December 1976 and became Transamerica Airlines on October 1, 1979. This aircraft was wfu and stored at Marana Pinal Airpark in Arizona. It was later bought by Northwest Territorial Airways as C-GNWD in June 1983, later being sold to Falcon Cargo as SE-IVS on September 28, 1986. (Michel Anciaux)

Falcon Cargo Lockheed L-188CF SE-IVS at Malmö Airport, Sweden, on June 28, 1988. Operating for the Swedish Postal Service, this aircraft was leased to Hunting Cargo Airlines as EI-CHW in May 1993. It was wfu at East Midland Airport, UK, in 1996 and was broken up in August 1998.

TAME Lockheed L-188C HC-AZJ at Quito Airport Mariscal Sucre Airport, Ecuador. October 28, 1977. This aircraft was delivered to Qantas as VH-ECB (msn 2004) *Pacific Explorer* on October 30, 1959, and was sold to Air California on August 18, 1967, as N385AC. It was then bought by the GATX-Boothe Aircraft Company on December 4, 1968, and directly leased to Air California. It was then sold to Aircraft Holdings Inc on March 19, 1969, and bought by F. B. Ayer Inc on November 7, 1969, which leased to Universal Trading Corporation on December 17, 1969. It was wfu and stored at Fort Worth Airport in 1970. The aircraft returned to F. B. Ayer on January 12, 1972, and was subsequently leased to Intermountain Aviation. It was bought by Wharfca Inc in November 12, 1973, and leased to TAME as HC-AZJ in December 1973.

This TAME Lockheed L-188C is flying past the Cotopaxi volcano, one of the highest volcanoes (5,911m) in Ecuador, on its way from Quito Airport to Guayaquil Airport. This aircraft was bought by TAME on August 6, 1974, as FAE2004/HC-AVJ named *Pichincha*. During a flight on September 4, 1989, from Quito Airport to Tulcan Airport, in the north of Ecuador, the aircraft's left gear warning light remained on after take-off. A gear-up landing was carried out at Taura AFB, in the southeast of Ecuador; the Electra was damaged beyond repair, but all seven crew and 92 passengers were saved. The probable cause of the warning light was that the bolts on the front gear doors were stuck because of a stuck support rod.

Flamingo Airlines Lockheed L-188C N31231 at Nassau Airport in March 1973. This aircraft was delivered to Tasman Empire Airways as ZK-TEA on October 15, 1959 (msn 2005). The company was renamed Air New Zealand in April 1965, and it was bought by the California Airmotive Corporation on May 27, 1972. The aircraft was leased to Flamingo Airlines from June 1972 to November 1972, and then returned to the California Airmotive Corporation to be converted to L-188CF standard in December 1972. Formed in March 1971, Flamingo Airlines was a privately owned company that flew inter-island services in the Bahamas with a BAC 1-11 and a Convair 340. Two Electras, N172PS (msn 1109) and N31231 (msn 2005) were leased as services expanded to Miami and inter-island traffic increased. Flamingo Airlines was absorbed into the government-owned Bahamasair in 1973. The aircraft was bought by Fred Olsen Flyveselskap A/S as LN-FOI on September 11, 1973. (R.M Collection)

Fred Olsen Flyveselskap A/S Lockheed L-188CF LN-FOI at Schiphol Amsterdam Airport on August 9, 1989. The aircraft was bought by Voksenkollen Hotelcompani A/S on January 1, 1990, and leased to Fred Olsen on January 1, 1991. It was wfu at Oslo Fornebu Airport in February 1997, then later flown to Coventry Airport, UK, for storage in December 1997. It was later bought by Worldwide Aviation service Inc for parts.

KLM Royal Dutch Airlines Lockheed L-188C PH-LLC *Mars* at Amsterdam Schiphol Airport on May 28, 1968. First flown on October 24, 1959, this aircraft was delivered to the KLM as PH-LLC (msn 2006) on November 19, 1959. The aircraft left KLM after nine years of service after being bought by Universal Airlines as N853U in November 1968, after which it was converted to L-188CF standard. The Electra was repossessed by First National City Bank on May 4, 1972, and leased to Saturn Airways on May 5, 1972. Saturn Airways then bought the Electra on June 27, 1974.

Transamerica Lockheed L-188CF N853U at Miami Airport October 28, 1981. The aircraft was leased to Trans International Airlines in January 1986 and returned to Transamerica in July 1986. It was bought by Falcon Cargo on October 2, 1986, as SE-IVR, and was later sold to Hunting Cargo Airlines on May 29, 1993, as EI-CHX. Next it was bought by Channel Express on July 6, 1993, as G-BYEF. It was scrapped on December 14, 1998, and used by the Dart Group for parts at Bournemouth Airport.

Air Spray Tanker 484 Lockheed L-188C C-GHZI at Kamloops Airport, British Columbia, on August 17, 2020. Originally delivered to Qantas as VH-ECC on November 24, 1959, (msn 2007), this aircraft was bought by Air New Zealand as ZK-CLX on April 18, 1965. It was sold to California Airmotive Corporation on February 16, 1968, as N1968R and leased to Reeve Aleutian Airways on February 22, 1968. During a flight over the Pacific on June 8, 1983, en route from Cold Bay to Seattle, the number 4 engine propeller and gearbox separated, damaging the belly and control cables. The pilots managed to land safely at Anchorage Airport, Alaska, and the aircraft was subsequently repaired and returned to service. It was bought by Air Spray Canada in January 2001 and converted to a fire bomber and registered as C-GHZI. (Santiago Arias)

Air Spray Lockheed L-188C C-GHZI (484) at Kamloops Airport, Canada, on August 17, 2020. This aircraft is normally based at Prince George Airport and Williams Lake Regional Airport, from which it operates during the firefighting season. It is in Kamloops Airport to refuel with retardant while helping the Kamloops Avro RJ85s in fighting a large fire near Penticton, British Columbia. (Santiago Arias)

Qantas Australias Overseas Airline Lockheed L-188C VH-ECD at Tokyo Haneda Airport on October 29, 1960. Delivered to Qantas on December 3, 1959, as VH-ECD (msn 2008), this aircraft was leased to Trans Australia Airlines from December 3, 1959, until September 7, 1960. It was then leased to Air New Zealand from April 1, 1970, until April 1, 1971, as ZK-TED. Qantas ordered four L-188C Electras on April 1, 1958, for use on both domestic and overseas services. Only a year after the Electras were delivered, Qantas stopped the domestic flights and gave the aircraft to Trans Australian. One Electra was leased to Trans Australian for a short time, but the Electras were then used for flights to New Zealand and South Africa, also to Hong Kong, Tokyo, Manila (via Port Moresby) and Biak, Papua. Two Electras were sold to Air New Zealand in 1965 and 1970, respectively, and were used mainly on pool flights between Australia and New Zealand. The remaining two Electras were sold to Air California in 1967. (Peter Gates Collection)

Nomads Inc Lockheed L-188C N836E at Oakland Airport, California, in April 1972. This aircraft was bought from Qantas on April 21, 1971, as N836E (msn 2008). Nomads, a travel club operation formed primarily with General Motors' employees, purchased this single Electra from New Zealand. It flew worldwide on club charters and was bought by Mandala in October 1981. (R.M Collection)

Mandala Airlines Lockheed L-188C PK-RLG *Jaya Perkasa* at Jakarta Kemayoran Airport in August 1985. During a flight from Jakarta Kemayoran Airport to Padang-Tabing Airport in Sumatra, it appeared that the Electra's right-hand main gear wheels had separated, and the pilots decided to divert to Medan Polonia Airport in Sumatra for a wheels-up landing. During the landing, all the propellers broke off and the aircraft burst into flames after coming to rest. PK-RLG was damaged beyond repair, but all 45 passengers and crew were evacuated safely.

KLM Royal Dutch Airlines Lockheed L-188C PH-LLD at Paris Le Bourget Airport on June 17, 1963. Delivered to KLM as PH-LLD (msn 2009) *Jupiter* on December 16, 1959, this aircraft was leased to Air Ceylon on November 1, 1960, to operate the company's services to western Europe, which started in London via Amsterdam, Rome, Cairo, Karachi and finally Colombo. The aircraft was returned to KLM on November 1, 1961. (R.M Collection)

Air Ceylon Lockheed L-188C PH-LLD at London Heathrow Airport in August 1961. Air Ceylon was formed in 1947 after the Ceylon Ministry of Communications and Works purchased three Douglas DC-3s for this purpose. Initially, operations were between Ceylon (now Sri Lanka) and India, but services to London and Sydney were introduced in 1949 after the company entered into an agreement with Australian National Airways, and Ceylon bought two Douglas DC-4s for that service. In February 1956, the company leased a Lockheed L-749A in full Air Ceylon colors from KLM for the weekly Colombo to London service, which was replaced with a Lockheed L-1049G from KLM. (Peter Gates)

Air Ceylon Lockheed L-188C PH-LLD at Amsterdam Schiphol Airport in December 1961. (Ad Jan Altevogt)

Persian Air Services (PAS) Lockheed L-188C PH-LLD at Amsterdam Schiphol Airport in February 1962. From January 1, 1962, until March 10, 1962, KLM leased PH-LLD to PAS, in full PAS colors on the left side, and KLM colors on the right side. PAS leased this Electra for use on its long-range services to Europe and the Middle East. PAS was established in 1954, and by 1960, the airline flew passengers to major European cities including Geneva, Paris, Brussels, London and Amsterdam. On February 24, 1962, PAS and Iranian Airways merged to form the Iran National Airlines Corporation (HOMA), also called Iran Air. (Driek Zwaan/H.Sluyter)

Air Ceylon Lockheed L-188C PH-LLD at Paya Lebar Airport, Singapore, in November 1960. Returned to KLM on March 10, 1962, by PAS, the aircraft left the KLM fleet in February 1969 after being bought by Universal Airlines as N854U. It was converted to L-188CF standard in June 1969. First National City Bank repossessed the aircraft in May 1972 and leased it to Saturn Airways in the same month. It was bought by Saturn on June 27, 1974, a few years before the company merged with Trans International Airways to became Transamerica on October 1, 1979. The aircraft was leased to Interstate Airlines in February 1984, and sub-leased to Galaxy Airlines in July 1984. On January 29, 1985, Galaxy Airlines was flying from Philadelphia International Airport to Charlotte-Douglas Airport, North Carolina, with cargo, when the right-side main gear jammed in transit during the gear retraction following take off. The crew decided to divert to Dobbins AFB in Georgia, and a belly landing was made on a foamed runway. The Electra veered off the runway at 4,200ft past the runway threshold, and a fire erupted in the right-side main gear, and the Electra came to rest 70ft from the right side of the runway. All three crew members survived, but the Electra was written off. (Peter Gates Collection)

Air New Zealand Lockheed L-188C ZK-TEB at Melbourne Airport in January 1971. Originally delivered to Tasman Empire Airways (Air New Zealand) as ZK-TEB (msn 2010) on December 18, 1959, the aircraft was sold to California Airmotive Corporation in May 1972 as N33506 and converted to L-188PF standard in August 1972. The aircraft was bought by Nordair Canada as CF-NAX on September 12, 1972. It was wfu and stored at Cartierville, Canada in May 1976. (Peter Gates Collection)

Nordair Canada Lockheed L-188PF CF-NAX at Montreal Dorval Airport in September 1973. This aircraft was bought by American Jet Industries in November 1977 as N63AJ and was sold to Reeve Aleutian Airways as N178RV on April 4, 1978. It was then leased to Northwest Territorial Airways on November 1, 1984, and was re-registered as C-GNWC in April 1987. It returned to Reeve Aleutian in September 1988 as N178RV and was later bought by Electra Aero Inc on January 6, 2010, as N2RK. Buffalo Airways purchased the aircraft on August 5, 2010, as C-FIJX, and it was still active as a tanker in 2022. (R.M Collection)

KLM Royal Dutch Airlines Lockheed L-188C PH-LLG *Neptunus*. Delivered on February 25, 1960, as PH-LLG (msn 2014), this aircraft was leased to Martinair Holland on April 1, 1968, and returned to the KLM on January 1, 1969. (KLM Archives)

Martinair Holland Lockheed L-188C PH-LLG at Schiphol Amsterdam Airport in May 1968. Martinair Holland was operating extensive passenger and charter services, and used two Electras, PH-LLD and PH-LLG, both leased from KLM. PH-LLD was leased for various short periods and carried Martinair Holland stickers on top of the KLM colours, while PH-LLG was leased for ten months in full Martinair Holland colours and was purchased by Universal directly upon its return to KLM. (Ad Jan Altevogt)

Above: Atlantic Airlines Lockheed L-188CF G-FIZU arrives at Groningen Airport Eelde, The Netherlands, on June 30, 2009, with a feathering propeller because of an engine failure. (Kas van Zonneveld)

Right: A view from the cockpit of Atlantic Airlines Lockheed L-188CF G-FIZU at Airport Eelde on June 30, 2009. (Kas van Zonneveld)

Atlantic Airlines Lockheed L-188CF G-FIZU takes off at Groningen Airport Eelde on June 30, 2009. (Kas van Zonneveld)

Interstate Airlines Lockheed L-188CF N857U at Vancouver International Airport in September 1983. This aircraft was leased to Interstate Airlines in September 1984 and bought by the company in September 1985. It was sold to Falcon Cargo in October 1987 as SE-IZU and was leased to Hunting Cargo Airlines on March 16, 1993. It was bought by Hunting Cargo Airlines on May 20, 1997, as EI-CHY, but was soon re-registered as G-FIZU on December 22, 1998, for Atlantic Airlines. Channel Express chartered the aircraft from March 22, 1999, until October 4, 2001, and was bought by Atlantic Airlines on June 16, 2004. Buffalo Airways bought the aircraft in 2016 as C-GIZU, and it was stored and used for spare parts. (R.M Collection)

KLM Royal Dutch Airlines Lockheed L-188C PH-LLH at foggy London Heathrow Airport, December 1963. Delivered to KLM on April 16, 1960, as PH-LLH (msn 2015), this aircraft had been in service with KLM for eight years when it was bought by Universal Airlines on June 11, 1968, as N858U. It was converted into an L-188CF freighter with a main deck cargo door. The Electra was repossessed by First National City Bank on May 4, 1972, and it was leased to Saturn Airways on May 5, 1972. Saturn bought the Electra in June 1974. (R.M Collection)

KLM Royal Dutch Airlines Lockheed PH-LLH L-188C at the old Amsterdam Schiphol Airport in 1962 in the company's old color scheme. (Ad Jan Altevogt)

Universal Airlines Inc Lockheed L-188CF N858U at Langley AFB in May 1969. This aircraft was bought by Northwest Territorial Airways as C-GNWC in May 1984 and sold to Falcon Cargo as SE-IVT on November 28, 1986. It was re-registered as EI-CHZ in September 1993 for Hunting Cargo Airlines and later sold to Channel Express for parts in July 1998. Universal Airlines purchased KLM's fleet of surplus Electras and had them converted to cargo configuration by Lockheed Air Service. This fleet was used on Universal's extensive network of Military Airlift Command contract flights, which linked US military logistics centres. These operations ceased in May 1972.

KLM Royal Dutch Airlines Lockheed L-188C PH-LLI at Zaventem Airport on August 11, 1965. This aircraft was delivered to KLM on April 29, 1960, as PH-LLI (msn 2016) *Ceres*. After eight years, it left KLM and was bought by Universal Airlines as N859U on March 31, 1968, being converted to L-188CF standard in October 1968. The Electra was repossessed by First National City Bank on May 4, 1972, and leased to Saturn Airways on May 5, 1972, being bought by Saturn on June 27, 1974. On November 18, 1979, flight 3N18 departed Hill AFB, Utah, for an IFR cargo flight to Nellis AFB. While climbing from FL120 to FL130, the crew reported a loss of electrical power and requested no-gyro vectors and immediate descent clearance. During the recovery attempt, the stress limits of the Electra were exceeded, and it broke up in flight over Granger, just west of Salt Lake City, killing the three crewmen.

Trans International Lockheed L-188CF N860U at Dayton International Airport (Ohio) in June 1980. Originally delivered to KLM Royal Dutch Airlines as PH-LLK (msn 2017) *Pallas* on May 14, 1960, this aircraft was sold to Universal Airlines as N860U on March 9, 1968, and converted to standard L-188CF. The Electra was repossessed by First National City Bank on May 4, 1972, and leased to Saturn Airways on May 5, 1972, being bought by Saturn on June 27, 1974. Interstate leased the aircraft in April 1984, and the company bought the Electra in September 1985. It was then sold to Air Traffic Service Corporation in October 1985 and leased back to Interstate Airlines, returning to Air Traffic Service Corporation in May 1987. It was next purchased by JBQ Aviation on November 30, 1987, and leased to TPI International Airways, which then bought the aircraft in August 1989 and re-registered it as N361WS in December of that year. It was wfu at Tinker AFB, Oklahoma, in September 1990 and broken up in September 1991 for parts for Channel Express in the UK in October 1991. (R.M Collection)

Garuda Indonesia Airways Lockheed L-188C PK-GLA *Palau Bali* at Paya Lebar Airport in September 1969. This aircraft was originally delivered to Garuda Indonesia Airways on January 14, 1961, as PK-GLA (msn 2020.) In total, Garuda purchased three Electras L-188Cs to replace its Convairs 240s, 340s and 440s on its longer domestic routes and those to other Far Eastern points, with jets being used for the longer international routes. Although one aircraft (PK-GLB (msn 2021)) was lost in an accident, the other two were flown continuously until 1972, when they were withdrawn at Jakarta Kemayoran Airport. (Peter Gates Collection)

Copa Panama Lockheed L-188C HP-640 departs Barranquilla Airport, Colombia, on April 30, 1976. This ex-Garuda aircraft was bought by the National Airmotive Corporation on May 4, 1973, as N320CA and sold to the California Airmotive Corporation on May 25, 1973. Copa Panama purchased the aircraft on May 3, 1974, as HP-640 and then sold it to Diamond M. Drilling Company on July 15, 1980, as N511PS. It was re-registered as N188DM on September 20, 1980, and re-registered again as N807DM in June 1981. Bought by Mandala Airlines as PK-RLI in July 1983, it was wfu and stored at Jakarta Kemayoran Airport in September 1989. It was bought by Air Spray Canada and used for spares in July 1995 and broken up in April 1997.

Garuda Lockheed L-188C PK-GLC at Jakarta Kemayoran Airport in September 1971. Delivered to Garuda on January 15, 1961, as PK-GLC *Danau Toba* with msn 2022, this was also the last Electra built. After 11 years of service, it was withdrawn from service and stored at Jakarta Kemayoran Airport in 1972. It was bought by California Airmotive as N322CA on May 12, 1973. (R.M Collection)

Panama Defense Forces Lockheed L-188C FAP400 at Panama City Tocumen Airport in November 16, 1983. This aircraft was sold to Miami Aviation Inc on October 23, 1973, and bought by the Panamanian Air Force as FAP400 on November 5, 1973. It was converted to L-188CF standard in May 1985 and re-registered as HP-1042 for the Panamanian government in 1985. Transafrik International purchased the aircraft in June 1987 as S9-NAF and based the aircraft in the Democratic Republic of Sao Tome & Principe and at Luanda in Angola. It was sold to Aerovias from Guatemala as TG-ANP in October 1991.

Transapel Express Colombia Lockheed L-188CF HK-3716 at El Dorado Airport on February 19, 1993. This aircraft was bought by Aerovias SA as TG-ANP in October 1991, but it was not taken up and was bought instead by SAVA Colombia as HK-3707X in February 1992. It was re-registered as HK-3716 in August 1992 and was leased to Transapel Express Colombia as HK-3716X from August 1992 until August 1994. It was returned to SAVA Colombia as HK-3716 and broken up at El Dorado Airport in March 1996.

Tony Jarvis shares his experience flying the Electra in the Canadian Artic

In 1974, I was launched into a career that would span 48 years and more than 21,000hrs of flight time across not only all of Canada, and also 24 percent of the world's countries. The majority of that time I was airborne, it was in a Lockheed product. Prior to starting in the Electra of Buffalo Airways in 2017, my time was spent flying the only Canadian civilian Lockheed Hercules around the globe. When the Hercules was sold, I was open to new opportunities with any operator. When Buffalo's Joe McBryan offered me a position on the Electra, I transitioned to another Lockheed aircraft, adding to the previous types I had flown.

The vast majority of the remaining airworthy L-188s are now in Red Deer, Alberta. Buffalo Airways owns seven, of which four are in active service. Two are Fire Suppression aircraft that work only in the summer months, helping to control forest fires in the Northwest Territories. The remaining two aircraft are the only freighter Electras in the world. The majority of our freight flying is done in the Canadian Artic, with the occasional southern sojourn into the more populated areas of Canada. Even though the aircraft was originally designed for the short- to medium-range transport of passengers on paved runways, over the years these Electras have transitioned into rugged freight haulers landing on gravel runways in austere environments. As a Fire Suppression aircraft, it handles like a fighter, with the hydraulic-boosted controls making it quite nimble. The crew like the responsiveness of the Electra not only in its flight controls but also in its engines, which give almost instantaneous power when the situation gets tight. In the freighter world, this nimbleness is not required, however it is nice to know of its availability should it ever be needed. Our cargo flights are designed to be as boring as possible. The crew normally shows up two hours prior to loading and start with calculations for the flight. Since the aircraft now is "Two Crew," the pilots not only fly but also load and off-load with the assistance of the ground engineer that comes on every flight. You would think that in an aircraft of this size, designed for a much larger crew than that with which we work, the workload would be too much for the pilots alone. However, this is not the case. With our excellent technical training and the experience of the captains, these extra duties have proven to be quite manageable. Furthermore, the aircraft cockpit was changed so that important system controls are accessible to the pilot, and flight training was adjusted to ensure safety of flight in two-crew environment.

The Electra accommodates standard 88x108in sheets on which four wood cargo pallets can be placed and secured. Mine site loads are fairly standard and vary from explosives to food, and occasionally an awkward load, for example metal access stairways, appear. We have often said, "if it fits in the door, we can make it fly" and "give it to Buffalo, they'll take ANYTHING!" After the Electra is loaded and the numbers are rechecked, the flight continues routinely to its destination. With the onset of satellite navigation systems, most of the approaches to runways in the Artic are now based on GPS, otherwise known as RNAV. This has been a game changer for us in the conditions in which we normally fly. Most people may assume that ice and snow are the major restricting factors in our operations. While that does hamper us during time on the ground, airborne concerns centre more on the wind during winter operations. In the Artic, there is really nothing to stop the wind once it starts to blow and, for days at a time, high winds will restrict forward visibility. It is somewhat reminiscent of flying in a milk bowl, where the sky melts into the ground in a solid palette of white. Weather reporting is fortunately very good, and that is normally not an issue. We also find flying at night to be an advantage, especially when the weather is bad. This allows us to see the runways better, as they are always well lit, and some are pilot-controlled for intensity. All this is not to say weather can't change in an instant, and sometimes does, completely going against forecast conditions. But, such are the hazards. Sometimes the flights are 'Pilot Self Dispatched' as communication can be difficult at some remote locations. However, thanks to technology, this is becoming rarer, and we can often talk to someone if things go awry during flight. With safety as a priority, operation of the Lockheed L-188 in the Artic is routine and quite enjoyable. Perhaps most fortunately, the aircraft is very warm.

Above: Buffalo Airways' main base at Yellowknife Airport, Northwest Territories. An Electra is there in old Buffalo colors.

Right: Captain Tony Jarvis in the cockpit of an L-188AF Electra on approach to Pond Inlet on the Northern tip of Baffin Island.

Above: The Electra is sitting at Igloolik Airport, Nunavut. The temperature outside is -40°C!

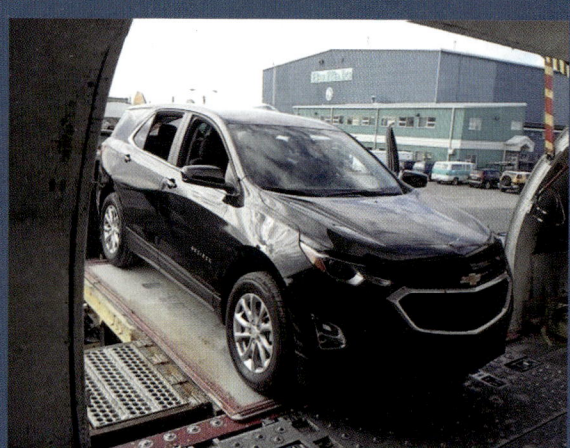

Left: A big car is being loaded in Yellowknife Airport, with the Buffalo Airport hangar in the background.

Below: Buffalo Airways Lockheed L-188AF C-GXFC is at Kugluktuk (formerly known as Coppermine) on the Coronation Gulf in the Canadian Artic.